A History of Scarisbrick

The first parish council, 1895.

The parish council, 1996 (inset, Councillor Jackson).

A HISTORY OF SCARISBRICK

MONA DUGGAN

Carnegie Publishing Ltd, 1996

Copyright © Carnegie Publishing, 1996

Text copyright © Scarisbrick Parish Council, 1996

First published in 1996 by
Carnegie Publishing Ltd
18 Maynard Street, Preston

ISBN 1−85936-040-8

Typeset by Carnegie Publishing, 18 Maynard St, Preston
Printed and bound by Bookcraft (Bath) Ltd

Contents

Illustrations

Abbreviations

T.H.S.L.C.	Transactions of the Historic Society of Lancashire and Cheshire
R.S.L.C.	The Record Society of Lancashire and Cheshire
C.N.W.R.S.	The Centre for North West Regional Studies
V.C.H.	*The Victoria History of the County of Lancaster*, eds W. Farrer & J. Brownbill
P.R.O.	Public Record Office
C.R.O.	Chester Record Office
L.R.O.	Lancashire Record Office

FOREWORD

CARISBRICK PARISH COUNCIL takes great pleasure in the publication of *A History of Scarisbrick*, which represents the culmination of a year of celebrations to mark the centenary of the Parish Council.

Scarisbrick Parish Council, like many others throughout England and Wales, came into being through the 1894 Local Government Act, which, far from being a rather dry and dusty piece of legislation, took over a year to pass through Parliament and was subject to over 800 amendments. The main cause of this vociferous opposition was the proposal to create parish councils which were seen as a threat to the established order of local affairs. One hundred years later it seems difficult to imagine that an organisation that now seems to many to be the embodiment of the establishment, should have been so controversial.

Scarisbrick Parish Council held its first meeting on 7 January 1895 and has been meeting more or less regularly ever since. In the years running up to the centenary the Parish Council determined that it should mark the one hundred years of its existence and many ideas were discussed. A few were not adopted but many others came to fruition; some were individual events which may, however, live on in people's memories (the two performances of *The Secret Garden* by The Storytellers or the Songs of Praise in Scarisbrick Hall that replaced the annual civic service). Others had more tangible outcomes that it is hoped will continue to be appreciated, such as the Competition Cups donated to local bowls, snooker and golf clubs, or the two public seats positioned in the parish.

Some took the form of gifts including the aerial photographs of the Village Hall and the contribution to the Senior Citizens' Christmas meal. A tea towel depicting local buildings was commissioned; whether these became a memento or served a practical household function was left to the purchasers – perhaps those that remain may even become family heirlooms! Some projects involved residents of the parish –

volunteers planted trees donated by the Parish Council in the grounds of the Village Hall where they should reach full maturity when another one hundred years have passed. The Parish Council's annual grants to the three local primary schools took a centenary-related theme, including the burying of a time-capsule at Pinfold.

Perhaps the most impressive of the community efforts sponsored during the year was the production of a tapestry which again depicted local buildings and scenes. The panels were designed and embroidered by many individuals so that the complete tapestry is truly a community venture. It has been much admired since it was put on display in the Village Hall; the Parish Council is grateful to both the Village Hall committee for providing a site where many people will see the tapestry and to Scarisbrick Women's Institute for providing a light to ensure they will see it clearly!

In these diverse ways the Parish Council celebrated its centenary, but the boldest resolution was to commission a history of Scarisbrick. One of the members of the Council, Councillor Mrs Edwards, had previously published a short history with many fascinating photographs, but that was no longer in print and the Parish Council felt that a longer, scholarly, but readable account would be of great interest. Fortuitously, Dr Mona Duggan was recommended to the Parish Council. Dr Duggan lived locally and had researched histories of neighbouring areas and she readily agreed to undertake this new challenge.

The Parish Council approached local firms for sponsorship, and is grateful to Halliwell-Jones Ltd, Kershaw's Frozen Foods, Ormsby's of Scarisbrick and Rushton's Nurseries for their support of this venture. Our thanks are also due to the publishers for their help and support. A final expression of gratitude must be made to the Clerk of the Parish Council, Mr John Cotterall, who took up the position shortly before the centenary year. His enthusiasm and determination were essential to the completion of this and the many other activities undertaken during the year.

The readers of *A History of Scarisbrick* will make up their own minds on its interest and value, but the draft read by members of the Parish Council was enthusiastically received. Dr Duggan has combined the scholarship of original research with a style that will enthral readers who wish to know more of the story that has led to the present parish of Scarisbrick and its several settlements. The Council is sure that this history will remain a definitive work for many years to come – perhaps until Scarisbrick Parish Council celebrates its next centenary.

Richard Small,
Chairman, Scarisbrick Parish Council
June 1996

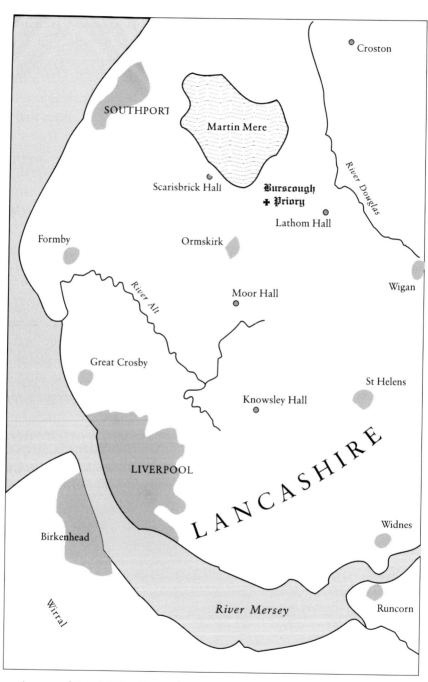

1. A map of South-West Lancashire.

Introduction

OWADAYS many people know Scarisbrick as a green oasis of woods and farmland to be crossed as they commute between one or other of the sprawling urban developments around her borders. The unspoilt parish stands astride the fertile lowlands of the South West Lancashire plain surrounded by huge settlements that have grown as a response to forces far removed from their roots in this once remote district of Lancashire. Although Scarisbrick has retained its rural character, these developments around its perimeter inevitably had an impact on its progress.

To the south the bustling city and seaport of Liverpool has probably exerted the largest influence on the development of Scarisbrick in the last three hundred years. The needs of that vast population dictated which direction the agriculture of the area should follow. Bootle, too, first as a hunting ground then as a resort and residential area in the nineteenth century, also made demands for produce from the rural area. Burscough on the eastern rim, rapidly extending from a village into a busy township with the coming of the canal and railways, turned to the area for supplies. Then to the west, the old fishing village of North Meols and later Southport, Ainsdale and Birkdale attracted both visitors and residents, swelling still further the growing need for fresh vegetables.

Long before most of these towns came into existence, Scarisbrick made its own demands on its neighbour, the ancient town of Ormskirk, and in its own way influenced the development of that long-established centre of south-west Lancashire. Ormskirk church was the mother church of the parish to which Scarisbrick belonged – an ecclesiastical bond that was not broken until the mid-nineteenth century. Ormskirk also served the people of Scarisbrick as a legal centre in the years before the growth of Liverpool, but the town's most important function was as the main market for the area. For countless generations the people from Bescar, Drummersdale, Snape, Hurleston and all the tiny hamlets within Scarisbrick took their goods to Ormskirk market. This time it was the needs of the people of Scarisbrick that had an influence on the development of their neighbouring town. They needed a market for their grain, vegetables and meat, and they needed access to a large variety of craftsmen: tanners to produce leather from their animals' hides; shoemakers and cordwainers to fashion the leather into clothes or harnesses; ropemakers to produce every thickness of rope for their needs; coopers to make barrels for storage; potters to make vessels for them; and all kinds of smiths and wrights to use their individual skills to supply the needs of the country folk. Of course, some of these skills were available in Scarisbrick, but Ormskirk could provide a greater choice and as the demand grew, the larger town's economy altered to provide for the needs of Scarisbrick.

Yet somehow, despite interacting with the surrounding towns and villages, Scarisbrick has always stood aloof. Even today, although she continues to feed her neighbours, to allow them to cross her footpaths, to sail along her waterways, and to pollute her air with the fumes from their traffic, she still retains her identity.

Southport and its suburbs reach out for land for housing on the west; Ormskirk and Burscough are expanding on the east; only to the north where the great Martin Mere guarded her boundary until the late eighteenth century, are Scarisbrick's borders secure against threats of development. No doubt, the guardians of present-day Scarisbrick some-times wish that today's invading crowds could be persuaded to follow the example of Celia Fiennes who in 1689, 'avoided going by the famous Mere called Martin Mere . . . it being near evening and not getting a guide I was a little afraid to go that way it being very hazardous for strangers to pass by it'.[1]

In this history, I want to transport you back to those days when Scarisbrick was truly a very remote area, far away from any major route-way, an area to be shunned because of the dangers that lurked in its mossland. Certainly, members of the nobility and gentry crossed the area occasionally to visit one or other of the families who lived in the manor houses, but the lives of the ordinary folk of Scarisbrick were seldom affected by any great happenings; they were too busy fighting their own battles against the landscape and the elements. Nevertheless, it is the history of these people that I want to chart in these pages. The histories of great families have been chronicled many times, but my challenge is to present an account of life in Scarisbrick through the ages until the times when the older residents can contribute a record of their experiences. The more recent past will not be described, in case the book becomes tedious to those whose lifetime in Scarisbrick spans that period.[2]

Shakespeare gave us the quotation that 'all the world's a stage, and all the men and women merely players'. In this history, Scarisbrick is the stage and the men and women of the township are the players. Through its pages we will have the privilege of watching as scenes of their lives at various points in time are performed. Our entrance to this parade of the past is a collection of documents drawn up at the time for legal purposes, and if no documents exist, then we cannot gain access to that particular period. Consequently our history must be a series of episodes and a silent veil will be drawn over the undocumented times.

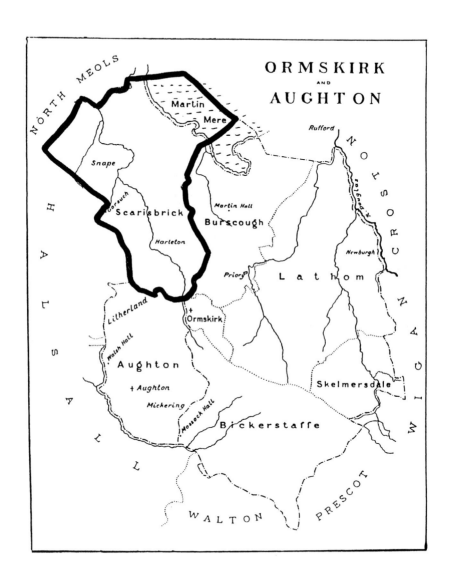

2. The parishes of Ormskirk and Aughton showing the township of Scarisbrick.

CHAPTER 1

THE EARLY HISTORY
OF THE TOWNSHIP

The medieval scene in Scarisbrick

HE EARLIEST WRITTEN ACCOUNT of local landholdings is
the Domesday Book, but it provides little evidence of the
existence of Scarisbrick. The only part of the township
mentioned is the eastern settlement of Harleton, later to
become known as Hurleston. 'Harleton and half of Martin' are valued
and recorded as being part of the lands of Uctred in 1066. Many
historians think that Uctred was an early lord of Lathom, but that
cannot be proved. During the reign of Richard I (1189–99), a later
member of the Lathom family by the name of Simon of Grubhead
granted part of his lands to his brother Gilbert who became known as
Gilbert of Scarisbrick and it is the activities of his family which provide
us with our first glimpses of life in the township.[3]

The earliest scenes are drawn from charters whereby Gilbert and his
immediate descendants Walter (c. 1229–c. 1260), Henry (died c. 1275),
Gilbert II (living in 1339) and Richard granted land to two religious
establishments, Cockersand Abbey and Burscough Priory. In their day,
such acts of piety were made on the understanding that the canons
would pray for the souls of the donors. Burscough Priory, founded in
1189 by the black canons and dedicated to St Nicholas, was funded at
its foundation by a grant of lands made by Robert, son of Henry of
Lathom, then head of the family that was to become the Derby family.
He granted the church in Ormskirk with all its lands to the Priory and,
as Scarisbrick is one of the six townships which comprised the parish
of Ormskirk, Scarisbrick passed from the control of the Lathom family
into the hands of the prior and canons of Burscough priory, and from
that time until the Reformation the people of Scarisbrick paid tithes to
the priory.[4]

Within the bounds of the parish were several manors held by secular

lords, whose lands had originally been granted to them by the lords of
Lathom. Scarisbrick township consisted of two manors; Scarisbrick and
Harleton or Hurleston, both held by military service of the Lathom
family. Thus, when the Lathom family was called upon to supply the
king with armed men, they would ask the Scarisbrick or Hurleston
family to provide the necessary money to equip a knight for the king's
service. As time passed this requirement altered and a rent was paid
and many years later the two manors became the freehold property of
the Scarisbrick family. We already have a fine account of this family
and the transfer of their lands from one generation to another in the
Victoria County History,[5] so it would be pointless to repeat the family
history. Nevertheless, members of the family will appear in this account
at various times, as they supervised law and order through their court
leet, provided homes and schools, churches and almshouses for their
tenantry, and generally kept a watchful eye on the welfare of the
community living in Scarisbrick.

Several of the transactions made between the prior and the lords of
Scarisbrick, Hurleston and Martin, and recorded in the respective cartularies,[6] give us descriptions of the landscape of Scarisbrick, but as many
of the place-names are unfamiliar to us, it is impossible to pinpoint
many of the features. The cartulary of Burscough Priory confirms that
the landscape of Scarisbrick was then dominated by ditches and dykes.
Virtually all the boundaries within the township are marked by some
kind of watercourse. Who dug all these ditches we have no idea, but
certainly the economy of the district depended on their efficient maintenance. In the days before any pumping system, the watercourses were
wider than today, and in fact there are several mentions of Harleton
ferry, so presumably that stream was too wide to be crossed by a simple
'platt' or footbridge. There are many familiar place-names in the charters of the thirteenth century. These tiny hamlets – or perhaps only
farmsteads – include Renacres, Snape, Mescar, Shaw, Aspinwall and
Martin, while other place-names such as Gosford Syke, Blakelache and
Otecroft, may well have been the early form of Gorsuch, Black Moss
and Otterstye. Two farmsteads, Miggehalch and Menehey are mentioned, and so the present-day Midge Hall and Meanygate can claim a
very early date for their origin. The present-day farmsteads of these
names may not be on the original sites, but may have moved on to
reclaimed mossland at a later date.

There are very few clues to the way the tenants made a living. Pastures, meadows and oak woods confirm that they kept animals, but pigs are the only ones actually mentioned. These pigs belonged to Stephen de Martin, who between 1243 and 1260, had the right of pannage in certain woods. For the right to allow his pigs to forage, he paid half a pig annually to his lord. Stephen's lands included Miggehalch (Midge Hall) and his rent was a quarter of a pound of pepper and a quarter of a pound of cummin as well as a rent in money. At this date, both these spices would be imported from the Mediterranean lands and so were valuable. Of course, in later years a 'peppercorn rent' meant that no payment was to be made. In two of the grants made by Roger of Harleton, a granary is mentioned and a place-name – Graynethake – suggests that some kind of cereal was grown in the area. Another place-name, Flaxriding, indicates that flax was grown in clearings on the wetlands, and the mention of kilnsteads and pits suggest that the clay from outcrops in the area was used for making pottery.

Cockersand Abbey's charters give us another glimpse of the township. In the grant dated sometime between 1200 and 1246, Robert of Hurleston gave the canons an acre and a half 'in the heart of Hurleston townfields'. This description provides evidence that the tenants of Hurleston held strips in the townfield. The three-field system of leaving one field fallow each year did not operate in this part of Lancashire, but nevertheless, the good land was divided in strips among the tenantry. Another charter mentions Robert the miller, who would grind the oats and possibly the wheat grown on the strips to produce oatmeal and flour. The toft or smallholding of the miller was near the first field dale (dole) – the first part of the field doled out or divided among the tenants. In this same charter the canons are given an acre in Peasacres – probably another divided townfield where various food crops were grown. Again the right of pannage for the tenants' pigs is mentioned.

Thus the charters provide us with a picture of two settlements on the higher ground south of Martin Mere: Scarisbrick, a more scattered community and Hurleston, a group of small farms clustered around the Hurleston Green area. There were possibly three townfields in both manors where each household had a share of the most productive land. On one of these fields cereals were grown, most probably oats and barley which thrived in the colder climate of northern England. The other produced vegetable crops, and the third on the lower wetter ground was used for growing flax or hemp. No doubt the cottagers prepared linen thread and wove their own garments of linen. Within both of the manors were large areas of common pasture where the tenants allowed their cattle, sheep and horses to graze, while surrounding the settlement and on the poorer ground, were extensive woodlands where the pigs could forage. These woodlands also provided the 'twigs' from which the tenants made baskets – as they continued to do until the twentieth century. Their animals provided them with wool and leather for clothing, and meat for food. If they had any surplus of grain, vegetables, leather or yarn, they took it to sell at the crossroads in Ormskirk. There, an embryo market functioned long before the actual charter was granted in 1286 allowing the canons to charge tolls from all those attending the market.

The lords of all the mereside manors had the right to fish in the mere. In fact in the fourteenth century the lord of North Meols challenged this right in the court, claiming that two Rufford fishermen were catching 'his' bream, but the justices of the peace ruled that the right to fish the waters of the mere was held in common by all the townships around the mere.[7] The lord of the manor of Scarisbrick conveyed his right to the fisheries in the mere to certain of his tenants, and allowed them to fish commercially, while the other inhabitants were free to catch fish for their own consumption using rods and lines. The tenants also caught eels in many of the ditches to supplement their diets. In fact one of the brooks is known today as Snig Pot Brook (Eel Pot Brook) – near Bullens Lane. Evidently it was one of the places where eels could be trapped. No doubt waterfowl and their eggs would be eaten by the less law-abiding townsfolk, even though the birds were officially the property of the lord of the manor.

The Manor Houses

1. *Scarisbrick Hall*

There are no records containing descriptions of the manor houses before Tudor times. It was thought that the original site of Scarisbrick Hall was moated, not particularly for defensive purposes, although a moat would deter thieves, but mainly to provide both a drainage system to carry water away from the foundations of the building, and also a sewage system to remove waste from the hall. However, archaeological excavations conducted in 1960 on the trenches (about 165 yards away from the present site of the house), cast doubt upon this theory. It was found that the ditches had been dug at different dates, and it was thought that the moat was in fact a fishpond to provide the house with fresh fish. Whether that was really necessary with Martin Mere nearby is doubtful. Nevertheless, that was the conclusion drawn by the archaeologists.[8]

The will of Thomas Scarisbrick, written in 1530, refers to his manor place with barns, oxen houses and houses of office. In the hall only six rooms are mentioned: a chapel, a chamber, a buttery, a larder, a kitchen and a brewhouse.[9] We also have a list of the property included in the manor of Scarisbrick in a deed dated 1546. At that time there were a hundred messuages (dwelling houses with their adjacent land) and forty cottages, a water mill, a windmill and a dovecote, forty tofts (small holdings), a hundred gardens and forty orchards, along with two hundred acres of meadow, a hundred acres of woodland, six hundred acres of moor, moss and turbary, a thousand acres of land, six hundred acres of pasture, a thousand acres of heath and part of Martin Mere.[10] Many of these acres were unenclosed land unfit for use except in the summer time if it dried out sufficiently to be used as pasture.

In the 1560s the lords of the manor decided that the hall was too small for their needs and in 1569, Edward Scarisbrick (1566–99) built a new hall on slightly higher ground a short distance away from the original hall. The inventory compiled on the death of Edward's successor,

3. Scarisbrick Hall in the early nineteenth century.

Henry in 1608, gives us an idea of the extent of this property.[11] The actual living quarters included a hall, a parlour, a larder, buttery and kitchen, a great chamber, a new chamber, a chamber over the buttery, a chamber over the larder, the servants' chamber, the maidens' chamber, the gatehouse chamber, three 'prentises' and a chapel. From this list we can infer that the great hall formed the central axis of the building and the great chamber was over it. Adjoining the hall would be the parlour at one end with the new chamber over it, and at the other end of the hall would be the kitchen, larder, buttery and bakehouse with the other chambers over this working area. The gatehouse chamber would probably be over the projecting porch area and the 'prentises' would be additional bedrooms probably situated in the gables projecting from the central portion of the upper floor. An etching made of the hall about 1800 gives us a view of this timbered building after it had been covered in some kind of rendering. Of course, by this date many alterations had been made inside the hall, but the exterior – particularly of the central part – was probably very similar to the original. According to a description of the house made about the same time as the etching, there was a datestone over the porch with the name of Edward Scarisbrick, the date – 1569 – and the family coat of arms carved on it. Among the carvings in a room used as a dining room in the nineteenth century were the initials E.S. and the date of 1595, suggesting that the room was a slightly later addition to this second hall.

Other parts of the property listed in this early inventory include the milk house, the old and the new mill. The existence of an old mill at this time is interesting as it has almost the identical contents as the new mill, which suggests that both mills were operating at the same time. Although no canvas sails are listed with either of the mills, the inclusion of a windmill in the property of the manor (1546) suggests that one of these mills was a windmill and one was a watermill. The millers evidently slept in the mill, for in both mills beds are listed, a feather bed in the old mill and a chaff bed in the new one. In 1699 plans were made for another watermill 'near unto the Hall of Scarisbrick'. An agreement was made between Robert Scarisbrick and John Crook whose land would be affected by alterations made to the watercourses.[12] The necessary changes were listed and permission was granted by John Crook for Robert's workmen to have access to his land to construct the new ditch which was not to exceed ten feet in breadth. A sluice, not exceeding six foot in height, was to be erected in the old brook to divert the water into the new ditch and banks were to be built to prevent any flooding. Three bridges were to be built of stone or bricks 'strong enough for loaded carts to pass', and the whole scheme had to be completed within forty days. These works were located to the south east of the hall and extended from John Shaw's orchards – possibly now the Shaw Hall caravan site – to Dam Wood on Hall Lane. It is difficult to identify exactly which ditch was dug, because there have been so many subsequent drainage schemes and the canal has been imposed on the whole system. Crook was granted ten shillings a year by the agreement and the right to have 'corn ground at the said water milne hopper free, next after the corn of the said Robert Scarisbrick or his heirs'. This privilege would have been a great asset for Crook for once the corn was harvested, every tenant wanted to grind his corn at the same time and, as it was compulsory for the tenants to use the lord's mill, it could be very frustrating waiting for an opportunity to use the mill.

The 1608 inventory gives us a second glimpse of local farming at the time. The animals included eight oxen, two bulls, fifteen cows, twelve calves, six horses, two mares, eight sheep, twenty-one pigs, eighteen geese and an unspecified amount of poultry. The crops in store included barley, oats, peas and beans, and hay for the animals. Wheat had already been sown at the time of the inventory (October) for the following year. Linen and canvas 'slippings' and two spinning wheels suggest that flax and hemp – for the canvas – were grown on the estate and the women were employed spinning it into yarn for the weaver. Indeed, a court leet presentation at Ormskirk in 1537 confirms that during Tudor times flax yarn was one of the products traded in Scarisbrick.[13] Thomas Banks and his wife had broken a contract to supply three clippings of flax daily to Peter Carter and were brought to the court to make restitution. Peter was probably a weaver whose earnings had been reduced by the lack of yarn. Altogether twenty-nine yards of canvas were listed in the 1608 inventory, probably woven in the township for use for sails or sacking. The nets and boats to be used for fishing on the mere were also mentioned, along with 'turffe' valued at five shillings. From these documents we get a very similar picture to that we drew from the cartularies. In fact, there had been very little change in the area's farming during the intervening five centuries.

A book, *Britannia Baconia or The Natural Rarities of Lancashire*, printed in 1661 gives us yet another similar glimpse of the agricultural economy. 'The soile is not very fruitfull, yet it breeds great number of cattle, that are of huge proportion, and have goodly heads and large spread horns. Here is also fish and fowle on the sea coasts in good plenty . . . and a competent increase of flax. Where the ground is plain, it is good for wheat and barley; that which lyes at the bottom of hills is better for oats.'[14] There was no mention in either the inventory or the book, of potatoes and the other root vegetables that were to dominate the agriculture of the area a couple of centuries later. The author of *Britannia Baconia* drew attention to a feature of life on the mosslands which was probably unfamiliar to a visitor to the area. He explained that 'the people use turfs for fire and candle both'. He also attempted to explain the origin of the many bog oaks found embedded in the mosslands, and wondered 'whether they be not subterraneous trees growing underground as well as plants and other creatures' – a plausible explanation, I suppose, before the days of scientific research.

In 1673 James Scarisbrick, the grandson of Henry, died and the inventory of his goods compiled for taxation purposes gives us more information about the house. It had been altered internally and possibly enlarged since the days of Henry, who was only twenty-four when he died, and so would not have kept a large household nor would have needed many bedrooms for a growing family. It is possible that preparations had been made by James for further extensions to the house or even for the building of another hall to the west of the existing one, possibly on the site of the present New Hall farm. Among the items are 'tymber framed for the new house'and 'timber intended for seelinge of the decedent's chamber and flowreinge at Newhall'. Certainly, a drawing room has been added or divided from the rest of the great hall, and more bedrooms and nurseries had been constructed – a sign of the growing need for privacy which emerged in society about this time.

Among the chambers is that of Mr Christopher Bradhaigh, the priest and schoolmaster, a relation of the Scarisbricks and a member of the Bradshaigh family of Haigh near Wigan. Strangely the schoolroom contains only various kinds of timber. Perhaps they were stored at one end of the room, or perhaps they may have been put there to disguise the true purpose of the room in case the local constable called to search the house for any signs of the teaching or practice of the Catholic faith, which was illegal during this period. Another indication of this kind of subterfuge was the fact that a large bed and a screen were listed 'in the false roof', a sure sign that the priest took refuge in that part of the building. It is also significant that the chapel listed in the previous inventory has disappeared and has been replaced by a room described as a dining room – catering for the Lord's Supper perhaps.

The farm's large stock is also more detailed. There was a very large flock of sheep, seventeen milking cows and a bull, as well as many bullocks, heifers and calves. Oxen and horses for drawing carts and farm implements are listed together with several other horses, mares and colts. Pigs and poultry complete the list of animals. Barley, oats and wheat are stored in the garners and barns, and 'wheat unthrashed' was stored in the new barn – evidently an extension built as the size of the crops increased. As the inventory was compiled in May, the wheat must have been threshed throughout the year as the need for flour arose. Oatmeal and groats were stored in the hall.

The hall continued unaltered until 1813 when it was renovated and refaced in stone. New windows were made, the porch was redesigned and 'gothic' details were added to make it comply to the fashion of the day. The hall's great rebuilding 1834–45 by Charles Scarisbrick and later in the 1860s by Lady Ann Scarisbrick under the guidance of the Pugin family is well documented, consequently it is unnecessary to repeat the details here.[15]

2. *Hurleston Hall*

Although we have no description of the very early manor house at Hurleston, we know that much of the building that was demolished in the 1920s, dated from the fifteenth century. The central hall was similar to the old hall at Rufford, and part of the east wing belonged to that period. The rest of the building was added about the beginning of the seventeenth century, making a ground plan in the form of an 'H'. The old hall was timber-framed on a massive wooden sill resting on a wall of wrought stone about twelve inches high. At half the height of the hall, the timbers were mortised into a wooden head-piece with a band of carved ornamentation along its length. Above that was a shorter row of upright timbers reaching the wall plate at roof level.[16] During the alterations in the seventeenth century, an upstairs floor was inserted

4. Hurleston Hall at the end of the nineteenth century.

into the old hall, and the timbered minstrels' gallery was incorporated into bedrooms. In the course of time, the weight of this additional floor damaged the external walls. A large bay window extending over two stories and built of brick with stone mullions, was also added to the southern aspect of the central hall. It is thought that at one time the building included a chapel, and certainly in 1873 human remains were moved to Ormskirk parish graveyard from a burial ground close to the hall.[17] The Hurleston family finally sold their estate in the 1730s to the Scarisbricks, and new tenants moved into what had become a farm-house. Throughout the following two centuries windows and fireplaces were altered to modernise the interior, but the framework decayed and in the 1920s it was thought to be beyond renovation. The hall was abandoned and later demolished.

3. Gorsuch Hall

As the cartularies record, Gorsuch was established as a small estate in the early thirteenth century, when it was granted by Walter de Scaris-brick to his younger son, Adam. It continued in the same family until 1742, when a descendant inherited the Scarisbrick estate and the two were combined.

In 1554 there was a dispute between two members of the local gentry, concerning the ownership of part of the lands of the Gorsuch estate.

Thomas Gorsuch had let the land in question to William Stopford of Martin Hall, but John Bold of North Meols disputed Gorsuch's ownership of the land. Despite the fact that Stopford was farming the land, Bold sent his men to mow the grass when it was ripe, and to carry away the crop. In the resulting court case, Stopford declared that 'a multitude of riotous persons came and cut the grass and later fifty persons came with swords, daggers and bucklers and carried away a hundred loads of hay to the value of fifty pounds'. Mr Bold denied the accusation and said that the men were carrying only scythes, pitchforks and rakes, and that he had sent so many men in order to harvest the crop while the weather was fine. As the land remained in the hands of the Gorsuch family, Queen Mary's court must have found in their favour.[18]

The actual hall must have been similar in size and lay-out to both the early Scarisbrick Hall and Hurleston Hall. A survey made in 1655 describes it as having a hall, kitchen, larder, two butteries and seven other lower rooms, while upstairs there was a long room called the chapel chamber – probably over the central hall – four other rooms, and four closets. Judging by the number of rooms, Gorsuch was then the largest of the three halls. Outside was a range of outhouses including a decayed mill house, a kiln house of six bays, a barn of five bays, and nine other bays of outhousing. The milking yard, fold, orchard and rabbit warren provide further evidence of the extent of the farming activities around this estate.[19]

The survey was made when the estates of Royalists were confiscated following the civil war, and shortly afterwards the Gorsuch family paid £302 11s. 0d. to recover their estates from the treason trustees. Significantly in 1664, the hearth tax returns record that they paid tax on only six hearths, suggesting that the hall had been split into two or more dwellings in an attempt to recoup some of the money paid to the trustees. However, the family fortunes were improved in 1667, when James Gorsuch married into a wealthy Yorkshire family, the Methams of Metham, and received a marriage portion of £400. This James was the son of Edward Gorsuch and Mary Eccleston, and it was through this connection with the Eccleston family that the Gorsuch and Scarisbrick estates were united in 1742.[20]

Unfortunately Gorsuch Hall was totally destroyed by a disastrous fire in 1816. All that remains now to perpetuate the memory of a once large estate, is the name of Gorsuch Lane and the farmhouse built in the nineteenth century.

The impact of the Civil War on Scarisbrick

It is very difficult to discover exactly what was the attitude of the people of Scarisbrick to the Civil War. Several historians have attempted to make generalisations about the pattern of support received by each side; some suggest that the people of lower social status supported the Parliamentarians while the gentry supported the Crown; others suggest that most of the lower classes supported their manorial lords; others declare that support was based on religious allegiances – the Royalists were Catholic and the Parliamentarians were Protestant; and yet others are of the opinion that most of the lower classes were neutral.[21] Unfortunately we have very little local documentary evidence to throw light on the problem, but what we have gives a confusing picture and suggests a very mixed pattern of support.

Certainly, the allegiance of the Scarisbrick family to the Royalist cause was never in doubt. Edward Scarisbrick was described as a 'Papist in arms' during the First Civil War and was involved in the battles for Liverpool. This town was the centre of fighting in the early 1640s. In May 1643 Prince Rupert attacked the Parliamentarian forces established in the town and expelled them, and then in 1644 the tables were turned, when the Royalist garrison under Sir Robert Byron was besieged and forced to surrender to the Parliamentarians on 1 November.[22] During the fighting, the town was virtually destroyed and so in 1645 Parliament made an order that the town was to be rebuilt using five hundred tons of timber taken from the estates of their leading opponents. Consequently, hundreds of trees were felled in the grounds of Edward Scarisbrick, along with others from the estates of the Earl of Derby, Lord Molyneux and Charles Gerard. Four years later, the Commonwealth resolved that reparation amounting to £10,000 was to be paid out of the estates of Papists in arms. Again that included the Scarisbrick estate together with those of the Gerards at Bryn, the Blundells at Crosby, the Blundells at Ince, the Chorleys at Chorley and the Fazakerleys at Walton.

The Gorsuch family, also supporters of the king, suffered during the war when their house was ransacked and plundered.[23] Later, under the third Confiscation Act of 1652, the lands belonging to James Gorsuch, described as 'a Papist delinquent' and a Royalist supporter, were declared forfeit and were sold to George Pigot and William Smith. However, after the restoration of Charles II, James Gorsuch successfully regained his lands and embarked on the struggle to restore his estate to its pre-war condition.

Although the gentry suffered these severe penalties for supporting the Royalist cause, the ordinary people of Scarisbrick who were probably far too concerned about their crops and daily life to give much active support to either side, also endured hardship as a result of the war. Their crops were raided, their trade was disrupted and they suffered outbreaks of plague brought into the region by the soldiers. Four petitions presented to the justices of the peace at the Quarter Sessions give us a glimpse at four different aspects of the situation – and perhaps some indication as to where the loyalties of the ordinary folk of Scarisbrick lay.

The first, presented in 1646, concerns Gilbert, the eldest of the eleven children of William Sephton of Scarisbrick.[24] He served as a Parliamentarian soldier under Colonel Moore when Liverpool was taken by Prince Rupert. Gilbert was taken prisoner and 'carried away' by the Royalist forces. As the expedition passed through Scarisbrick on the way to York, the soldiers took a pair of 'shod' wheels and a new turf cart from Gilbert's father, William Sephton. Although they had a warrant authorising the constable of Scarisbrick to provide this equipment, Sephton received no payment from either the soldiers or the constable. In the end he appealed to the justices to order the constable to collect the money and to pay him. This was done, but not before he had struggled for months without essential equipment and without money to buy replacements. Although we have no proof, it could be argued that the constable's long delay in reimbursing Sephton was the result of the differing allegiances of the two men, or possibly the constable was only trying to conserve the funds of the township.

The second petition in 1646 was presented by Robert Hesketh, who had been constable of Scarisbrick, but was taken prisoner for not paying the Government the full amount of money he had been ordered to collect in taxes from the township.[25] His explanation involved two widows who lived in Scarisbrick, and whose husbands had both been slain in Liverpool by the forces of Prince Rupert. Both Colonel Moore and Colonel Egerton had agreed that the two widows, who had pleaded extreme poverty, should not be asked to pay their part of the assessment, a tax imposed by Parliament. Knowing this, the constable had not collected the money from them. This left him with a collection that was less than the original assessment and so, when the senior collectors came for the money, he was imprisoned because of the shortfall. In desperation he paid the widows' taxes himself and then presented his petition for restitution to the justices. No doubt he was granted it, but not before he had endured imprisonment and the resultant loss of earnings while the case was proceeding. Although the political allegiance of the constable in this case is unclear, it provides further evidence that the poorer classes were supporting the Parliamentarians by serving in their army.

The third petition (1650) gives us a sidelight on the local men involved in the actual battle for Liverpool against Prince Rupert.[26] Robert Shorliker of Scarisbrick is described as a 'listed' soldier, one of the local men enlisted by the Parliamentarians to swell their ranks against the Royalists. These men would have little or no training, and many would be paupers with no regular employment and no real inclination to fight. The petitioner described what happened in the following words:

> Robert Shorliker of Scarisbrick at the time of the Prince's coming to Liverpool, being a listed soldier under the command of Captain William Goulborne, did without his captain's consent or acquaintance . . . run away from Liverpool . . . with his said captain's coat and arms.

Evidently, Shorliker's commitment to the Parliamentarian cause was not sufficient to keep him on the battlefield, or to prevent him stealing his officer's possessions for his own gain. The petition goes on to blame the death of the captain and of many of his comrades on the captain's lack of arms, the consequence of Shorliker's theft and desertion. However, the petitioner's main concern was not to punish Shorliker for cowardice or theft, but in this instance to get restitution for the coat and arms. He wanted Shorliker to return the goods or pay the value of them to him. What happened next is not recorded, but we are left with a vignette of life among the ranks at the battle of Liverpool.

The last petition gives us a picture of the repercussions of the war in the depth of rural Scarisbrick, miles away from the scenes of fighting.[27] Despite the evidence of the last petition, some local men held very strong allegiances and this caused conflict within the local community which continued for many years after the war, as this case brought before the sessions in 1653 illustrates. Thomas Abram and Gilbert Waring were negotiating the sale of a bushell of oats, when Waring suddenly accused Abram of being a rogue because he had taken the engagement – agreeing to support the Commonwealth. Waring was so incensed at such a desertion of the Royalist cause that he struck Abram and his wife who was 'great with chyld' several times with a foot spade. The wife was hit on the head and Abram was man-handled so harshly that he 'made blood 8 days', and had not recovered from the incident twelve weeks later. Again we do not know the outcome of the petition, but nevertheless, it provides evidence of a continuing strong commitment of at least one member of the lower orders in Scarisbrick to the Royalist cause thirteen years after the outbreak of the Civil War.

Poverty and need during the reigns of the later Stuart kings

The restoration of Charles II did not mean that hardship disappeared from the township. Looting and raiding stopped after the war, but other endemic causes of poverty remained, forcing the townsfolk to appeal for help from the Quarter Sessions. Some of these petitioners had fallen on hard times through some disability; for instance in 1669 James Hutchen was described as 'a very poor and impotent man, not able to work, maintain and relieve himself'.[28] Others like Jennet Spencer, were old and infirm and 'so lame in one of her feet that she hath lyn under the care of her chiragon about eight months, not having anything to live upon, but the charity of her neighbours';[29] or like Ellen Holme (1674) who was also poor and weak, not able to work and without timely relief . . . [was] . . . like to perish'.[30] They all received some support albeit very little in our eyes.

The death of a spouse before the children were old enough to fend for themselves caused great difficulties for the surviving partner. In 1666 Thomas Parr was left with a little daughter and agreed to pay a neighbour, James Dalton forty shillings as year 'for to table'(feed and look after) the child. He fell behind with the payments and refused to pay the sixteen shillings he owed. The neighbour asked the overseers to take over the responsibility for the child, if the father continued to refuse to pay for her keep.[31] Similarly, Richard Hooton lost his wife and was left with four children under the age of eight. He asked for help in 1666 because he was unable 'by his own industry and pains though never so great to maintain and provide for them'.[32] Widows too, found it extremely difficult on their own. In 1650 Elline Blundell, a widow from Scarisbrick, lived in a poor cottage with her four children and had only about one rood – about a quarter of an acre – 'which would not any way support their necessities for one part of a year'. She claimed that she was compelled to let her children beg or they would starve.[33]

People suffering from illnesses and accidents which prevented them earning a living often appeared at the Sessions begging for help. One unusual case occurred in 1668 when Thomas Morecroft of Scarisbrick, a husbandman and servant to Edward Adamson, caught scrofula (tuberculosis of the lymphatic glands), a disease known as the 'King's Evil'. At that time it was thought that the only hope of a cure was to be touched by the king, so Thomas borrowed twenty shillings, 'having no friends nor any estate or other maintainence', and travelled to London. There he went to the Banqueting House, where he queued with hundreds of other sufferers to be touched. A group of surgeons directed the sick towards the throne to kneel before the king who stroked their faces. While this was in progress a chaplain recited the words, 'He put His hands upon them and He healed them'. When all the sick had been touched, they came up to the throne again in the same order to receive a gold 'angel' coin strung on a white ribbon. The king slipped it over their head while another chaplain said the words, 'That is the true Light who came into the world'. After a short service and a blessing the controller of the royal household brought a towel and a basin for the king to wash his hands. Towards the end of his reign Charles began to feel a revulsion at stroking the faces of people afflicted with scrofula and putting his hands on their swellings, so he decided to touch the gold pieces and instructed his chaplains and surgeons to put the talisman around the sufferers' necks.[34] Whether Thomas Morecroft was completely cured, we will never know. Certainly, the justices were convinced that his journey had been necessary, and they ordered the overseers of the poor for Scarisbrick to pay him the sum of 13*s*. 4*d*. to help him to repay his debt.[35]

Fire was an ever-present threat in the days of thatched roofs and open fires. As fire insurance had not been introduced in the seventeenth century, those who suffered loss by fire could only beg for help from the Church or from the overseers of the poor. In 1673 Gilbert Simpson of Scarisbrick asked the justices to recommend his case to the 'ministers of the Church' so that a 'charitable contribution' could be given to him from the various congregations. He claimed that he and his family were 'altogether destitute of any habitation or maintaynance . . . occasioned by a sad and dreadful fire that kindled in [his] . . . house and consumed all his substance'. The justices recommended the ministers to circulate a 'brief' around all the churches appealing for help for the family.[36] Another fire in Scarisbrick at a similar date, left Ellen Sumner, her husband and five poor children, including one both lame and dumb, without a home. The husband went to Ireland to seek relief – possibly from relatives – but returned with nothing. The overseers had refused to help while her husband was away, so when he returned, she appealed to the Sessions to keep them 'from perishing for mere hunger and want'. They granted her eighteen pence a week, but the document makes no mention of providing a house for the family.[37]

Homelessness was a great problem and in an earlier petition a homeless man, William Gill, and his family begged the justices to grant them an order enabling them to build a cottage and enclose an acre and a half of waste ground from the common land called 'Barrelsall Green' (Barrison Green).[38] A similar case arose in 1674 when William Rigby had been granted the right to build on the waste by the lord of the manor, but this must have been contested by John Barton 'and his confederates', who threatened to pull it down. Rigby appealed for an order declaring that he could legally build on the waste 'with the assistance of charitable neighbours'. Both of these appeals were granted.[39]

In each of these cases the petitioner explained that he was a long-standing resident in Scarisbrick, thus claiming settlement rights. If they had no such rights and could offer no security that they would not become chargeable to the township, homeless people were liable to be sent back to their original place of settlement. This often happened in Scarisbrick; for instance Bridget Gettenby and her son were sent back to Lathom in 1667, and in the same year William Barton and his wife were sent over the boundary back into Ormskirk.[40] Similarly in 1660 a one-time resident of Scarisbrick, Ellen Hesketh, was dispatched back from London 'from Constable to Constable' because she was 'visited with sickness' and needed help from the poor ley.[41] The valuable right to settlement was sometimes granted to those who could prove valid reasons for needing to change their place of residence. This happened in 1666, when Ann Barton came to Scarisbrick to care for her 'sickly and weak' married sister, Elizabeth Tasker. She lived peaceably in her sister's house and went so far as to build an extra bay on to the cottage for her own accommodation. She offered the town a good bond for their security and so the justices allowed her to settle in Scarisbrick.[42]

Not all the cases that came before the Quarter Sessions had such satisfactory endings. In 1684 Margery Hesketh, a 'very poor and ancient woman of a very honest and credible repute amongst her neighbours' gained the support of seventeen friends for her petition for a licence to sell ale within the township. Margery claimed it was the only way she could make a livelihood and avoid being 'cast wholey upon ye town'. The justices at the Sessions asked for sureties, but, when she could not provide any, they refused to grant a licence. However, she was not daunted and approached two other justices, whom she succeeded in persuading to overturn the former decision. She opened her house as an alehouse and allowed all kinds of disreputable people to stay 'all the night in the jolly exercises of gaming and drinking'. John Entwistle, one of the Ormskirk Justices of the Peace was horrified that 'gamesters frequented her house in the night time . . . men's sons and servants haunted the place at unreasonable times, it being an . . . obscure place'. He issued a warrant for the constable to fine her twenty shillings or to take her goods to that value, if she refused to pay the fine. However, the constable returned saying that all the goods in her house were not worth twenty shillings. At that, Entwistle ordered the overseers to help her and perhaps then, if she had some means of support, she would not need to run the alehouse. Realising that if she accepted help she would lose her profitable business, she refused their help. Entwistle had no alternative but to issue an order for the suppression of the alehouse. This was done and law and order returned to the township.[43]

Other cases concerning bastardy[44] and keeping the peace[45] indicate that life in Scarisbrick in the seventeenth century was anything but peaceful and uneventful. The constables were kept busy presenting offenders to the Quarter Sessions in either Ormskirk or Wigan, taking those found guilty to either the gaol in Lancaster or to the House of Correction in Preston, or even organising jurors to serve with the coroner at his court in Ormskirk whenever there was a sudden death in the township.

Leys and taxes

The constables' accounts of 1667[46] give us some idea of the taxes levied on the local community. National taxes included both the royal aid paid quarterly to the king, and another ley granted by the king for the Duke of York (later James II). These were the local contributions towards the expenses of the monarchy – for the royal household, for the upkeep of the royal palaces and so on. During the Civil War and when the royal brothers were living in exile during the Commonwealth, their income was drastically reduced, the royal residences were neglected and most of their possessions were purloined to meet the expenses of the new regime. Consequently it was necessary for Parliament to grant a new tax – this royal aid – to re-establish the monarchy and to restore it to its former condition.

In addition to these national taxes, similar collections were made for local causes. In 1667 these included taxes to help the maimed soldiers, most of them victims of the Civil War, and also to provide some assistance for those incarcerated in Lancaster Gaol and in the House of Correction at Preston. Local taxes also provided for the cost of maintaining beacons at Dalton and at Liverpool. These beacons were an old-established early warning system for use if a foreign power attempted to invade England. The fearful days of the Spanish Armada – eighty years earlier – were possibly, within the lifetime of some of the oldest inhabitants at this time, and so the need to pay for these defences was recognised and accepted. Finally, among local taxes collected by the constables in 1667, was one levied through the Quarter Sessions, to pay towards the repair of Lancaster Bridge. This bridge on the main highway into the town was used by the whole county and so, the cost was apportioned to each Lancashire township.

As well as all these various taxes the inhabitants of Scarisbrick also had to pay the constable's ley to re-imburse him for all his expenditure on warrants and on travelling expenses incurred in the course of his duties. The office of constable was an honorary post, so it was particularly important that his expenses should be met by the community. However, his accounts were not always paid without question; for instance in 1650 the accounts of Robert Shorliker, the Scarisbrick constable were challenged in court when he retired from his term in office. His accounts were duly examined and found to be correct. An order was made at the Quarter Sessions that the considerable sum – for that time – of £8 6s. 7d. owing to the constable was to be paid immediately.[47] It must have strained the resources of the elected constable to pay out that sum of money in the first place, and the delay of payment must have been very frustrating.

In 1703 the expenses of the constable of Scarisbrick were again under close scrutiny, and the court leet – the manor court – ordered that he must not claim more than sixpence for each time he went to Ormskirk on court business. This included his visits to meet various higher officials or to deliver taxes, lists of recusants or other lists such as the number of hearths in the houses of Scarisbrick for taxation purposes. The jury were determined that the administration of the manor should be efficient and above criticism. All the honorary officers were ordered to deliver their books, accounts and any money outstanding to the jury to be secured in the town's box within a fortnight of leaving office. If this was not done, they were fined the maximum fine the court could impose – thirty-nine shillings. Later, in the 1720s, the court defined exactly how much could be claimed in expenses by both the jurors and the officers. For the journey to Lancaster to appear at the assizes – probably involving overnight accommodation – they could claim six shillings and eight pence; for going to Preston county court they were allowed three shillings and fourpence; for going to Wigan the allowance was three shillings and for attending the court in Ormskirk one shilling. Whenever they attended the town's meetings, all the officers were to be allowed one shilling for out-of-pocket expenses.

Scenes from the Manor Court records

Most of the offences recorded in the records of the local court leets, or manor courts, were only the very minor ones, such as those committed by Thomas Balshaw and William Gobin of Snape and Henry Hill and Thomas Abraham of Scarisbrick, who appeared before the Court Baron of North Meols on 17 April 1640, accused of 'poullering in Wiche Diche betwixt the mere and the hall of Meales'. They had been beating the water with poles and spearing the fish, particularly the eels, as they swam away. They were fined six shillings and eight-pence — a very heavy fine imposed by the court to impress upon the inhabitants of Scarisbrick that the fish in those ditches belonged to the lord of North Meols and should not be caught without his permission.[48]

A more serious offence was committed by Richard Johnson of Scaris-brick in 1680. He was presented to the Court Leet of Ormskirk for bringing unwholesome meat for sale in the market. He was fined the large sum of 6s. 8d. by the Ormskirk jury, who were concerned that the reputation of their market for quality should not be under-mined.[49]

In general the offences brought before the Scarisbrick Court Leet were less serious.[50] In 1703 men stealing twigs from the woods for besoms or for thatching 'pricks' were prosecuted. John Barton was fined three shillings and fourpence in 1793 for 'being in a state of drunkenness and swearing and otherwise behaving in a very improper manner'. Although an order was made imposing a fine of 6s. 8d. against those who allowed visitors to stay in their homes without settlement certificates to indemnify Scarisbrick from any responsibility for their maintenance, there is no record of anyone being accused of that offence.

Similarly a fine of ten shillings was imposed on those who allowed their cattle or sheep to roam along the lanes in the township. In this case the pinder was empowered to fine the owners of the cattle and sheep on the spot without recourse to the court. Stray animals were impounded in various pinfolds — secure areas where the cattle were kept until their owners claimed them and paid the appropriate fine. Sturdy fences or walls were erected around the pinfolds to prevent the animals escaping, as was recorded by Robert Scarisbrick – 'Ye pinstocks sett up June 13th 1733' – in the book 'The Missive of Consolation' which he used as a diary.[51] One pound was on the site of the present

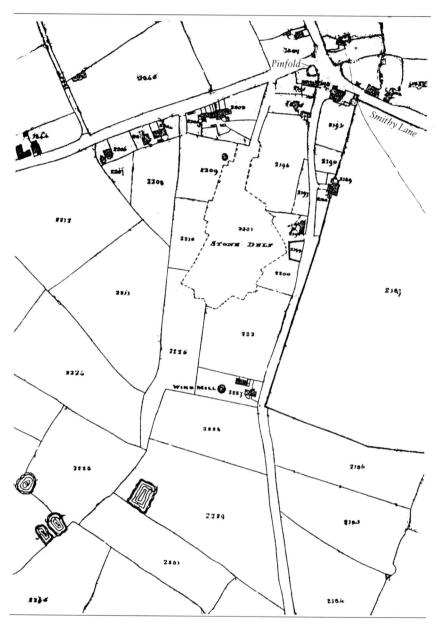

5. A portion of the 1839 tithe map showing the location of the pinfold (top right) opposite Smithy Lane.

Pinfold school and another was near Hurleston Green, but doubtless there were others in the western part of the township.

Not all the animals in the pounds had strayed on to the roadways, many belonged to other townships and had been found grazing on land belonging to Scarisbrick. For instance in 1722, the pinders for Martin Moss and Barrison Green, two areas of common grazing for the animals belonging to Scarisbrick township, were ordered to charge the owners of animals from other townships found grazing there, three shillings for a horse, two shillings for a cow and sixpence for a sheep. By 1792 these charges had increased to a shilling for each sheep and eight shillings for each horse or cow. Whenever animals strayed on to fields belonging to another farmer their owners had to pay a similar fine to the pinder.

Several orders were made to control the farming practices of the township. These were very necessary when much of the land was still held either in common or was farmed in large townfields. For instance, in 1702 the order was made that 'all that hold any meadowing in a meadow commonly called New Meadow, that they ditch ye brook betwixt May Day and Midsummer in pain of 6s. 4d.'. It was essential that such work should be controlled when the success of the community's hay crop depended on it. Similarly, it was important to regulate the peat mosses where inhabitants had the rights to graze their cattle and also to dig for peat. In 1703 it was ordered that animals grazing on the moss had to be tethered, so that they would not wander where the peat was cut and stacked. The officials known as moss seers were also ordered to keep all the roadways and gates on the mosses in good repair, and to open up the watercourses and gutters between the 'moss rooms' at the appropriate time to dry out particular areas of the moss ready for digging up the peat. The fact that the officials were given this task, indicates that the moss was a communal amenity divided among the inhabitants, with each family entitled to their share of the peat from whichever area or 'room' was ready for use.

In 1712 a deposition made during a court case concerning the ownership of Martin Mere describes in more detail the organisation of the fisheries in that part of the mere lying within Scarisbrick. The witness testified that 'there was anciently two fisheries between Parrock ditch and Dick's garden ditch' and these fisheries were let by the Scarisbrick family to tenants who were actually fish farmers, and who paid their rent in fish.[52] One particular farmer was quoted as paying thirty pikes and thirty pounds of eels a year for his tenancy. Later this rent was altered to a money payment. As we have seen from earlier documents, the Scarisbricks and their farmers kept boats, nets, snares and other 'engines and tackle' for taking and catching both the fish and the wild fowl on the mere. The farmers supplemented their income from the livestock by gathering reeds for thatching, by cutting grass for fodder and by digging out the bog oaks and moss wood for fuel. During the summer months when the land dried out, the farmers made use of the grass for grazing their horses and cattle. The witness in 1712 affirmed that the Scarisbrick's always had the right of catching and killing all swans and other wild fowl which were bred within the limits of the Scarisbrick part of the mere and also to take the eggs of such wild fowl 'to sell and dispose of at their pleasure'. The privilege of fishing with a rod in the Scarisbrick part of the mere was still granted to any of the tenants on the estate.[53] The hares, pheasants, partridges, 'conies or other game' belonged to the lord of the manor and at the court leet, the game keeper was appointed annually to protect the game and to seize any 'guns, bows, greyhounds, setting dogs, lurchers or other dogs, ferretts, nets, harepipes, snares or other engines for the taking 'of game.[54]

The maintenance of roadways, bridges and ditches was of utmost importance to the farmers for easy access to their holdings, and therefore was the main concern of the court leet throughout the eighteenth century. In 1704 drivers of packhorses and wagons were warned to keep to the ancient way to Hurleston and to 'lay a swift platt over the water course' – presumably a movable timber bridge. These 'platts' – flat bridges – were continually in need of repair. In 1708 the stone platt on Snig pott Lane (Bullens Lane) was recorded as 'ruinous lying in the snig pott'. Thomas Pemberton was ordered to erect a new one at his own cost. Similarly, on 2 November 1789 Thomas Burrows was ordered to widen a platt over the old mill stream in Gorsuch meadow before 25 December or he would be fined twenty shillings. In 1794 Thomas Ashurst was ordered to lay a proper footbridge with a handpole over the brook leading out of James Charnock's field into Woodbottoms under the penalty of ten shillings. These bridges were on private land, but if they had been on the public highway the cost of the platts and of paving stone for the roads was born by the township. When the bridge happened to mark the boundary between two parishes as on

Gorsuch Lane between Halsall and Scarisbrick, the cost was shared equally between the two parishes. Labour had to be provided by the inhabitants, and it was customary for all the townsfolk to provide six days unpaid labour each year towards the upkeep of the roads. Those with holdings worth over £50 per annum provided a cart and two men, while the less wealthy came to the site equipped with their spades.

Ditching was done at the cost of the landholders of the particular site, and of course, most of the persistent complaints about faulty ditching made to the court concerned the farmers on the lower land. The ditches around Pool Hey and the boundary with North Meols, and those around Jacksmere were frequently mentioned, while the Black Brook and the brook from the old mill to Martin Mere were a constant worry.

The draining of Martin Mere

Earlier attempts had been made to drain the mere by Thomas Fleetwood of Bank Hall in Bretherton in the 1690s. As we have seen from the inventories of the Scarisbrick family, the volume of farming both arable and pastoral had increased significantly in the seventeenth century. Consequently the mereside landowners decided to explore the possibilities of increasing their acreage of profitable land by draining the mere. They agreed to lease the lake to Thomas Fleetwood on 22 August 1694 for 'three lives and thirty-one years' and the whole arrangement was legalised by an Act of Parliament. The low-lying basin posed a great problem, because the mere naturally drained in two different directions: to the east into the river Douglas near Rufford, and to the west into the Wyke from where it flowed into another stream, the Pool, which took the water out into the Ribble estuary west of Crossens. Thomas Fleetwood decided to concentrate on the western drainage system, and employed over two thousand men to cut the main drain, 'the sluice', twenty-four feet wide from Crossens, across the saltmarsh, through bog land in North Meols, and across the mosses to the centre of the mere. Initially this was very successful and the waters rapidly drained away. However, the engineers knew that the spring tides, which rose higher than the waters of the mere, would reverse the flow and flood the mere basin with salt water. They solved this problem by constructing sluice gates which closed automatically when the sea level rose. For twenty years the land holders reaped the benefits of the newly drained land. The mosslands dried out sufficiently to be used as pasture for long periods of the year and the mere itself shrunk in size, releasing more land for use.[55]

Then the inevitable disputes arose between the mereside landowners as to who owned the drained basin. James, the tenth earl of Derby and Robert Scarisbrick complained that Thomas Fleetwood and the other landowners were obstructing attempts to divide the land. The two claimed that the largest area and the best quality of land was theirs by right, as they were the owners of the largest area of lake shore in the south and western part of the mere, the most fertile soil in the reclaimed area. Eventually, the dispute was taken to the County Palatine Court in Lancaster and witnesses were called to give evidence at the Wheat-sheaf Inn, Ormskirk, in May 1714.[56]

While the owners squabbled amongst themselves, a greater threat loomed over the sluice. The gates were gradually being silted up and were difficult to move. In 1714 Thomas Fleetwood authorised the raising of the floodgates' sill by twenty inches. Unfortunately this meant that a great deal of the original fall in level was lost and the drainage was less effective. Many of the newly drained pastures were seldom free of water. Although Thomas Fleetwood died in 1717, his executors continued his work and built a second pair of flood gates winged with stone walls nearer to the sea than the first pair. This improvement had very beneficial results. However, in 1750, Thomas Fleetwood's lease expired and five years later a strong tide washed the floodgates away and flooded the whole area again. The various landowners co-operated and re-erected the floodgates, but they were again soon choked with mud and the mere and its mosses continued to flood.

This was the situation in 1778 when Thomas Eccleston came to live at Scarisbrick Hall. He saw the potential of the drainage scheme and enlisted the help of John Gilbert an engineer from Worsley. John had been responsible for the construction of the underground canal which carried coal from the coal-face in the Duke of Bridgewater's mine at Worsley to the surface. He worked on that canal with James Brindley, who later took over and extended the canal over the Barton aqueduct to Castlefield in Manchester. Consequently, John had acquired great experience that proved to be invaluable to Thomas Eccleston. To avoid any further law-suits, Eccleston obtained leases for three lives from all but one of the landowners of the mere and set to work.

Three pairs of flood-gates were built in the sluice; the first, the seagates, to keep out the sea, the second, the flushing gates immediately behind the first but opening inwards towards the mere, and the stop-gates half a mile nearer the mere as a safety measure.[57] All three sets of gates had four paddles at the bottom three foot in length and two foot in depth, which could be drawn up by means of screws to flush away any obstacles that impeded their working. At low water all the gates were left open to allow the waters of the mere to drain out. As the tide rose the sea-gates were closed to keep the sea out. At high tides the flushing gates were closed, imprisoning a great quantity of water between them and the sea-gates. At low tide the flushing gates were opened and the rush of water cleared the channel down to the sea. In dry seasons the sea was allowed up to the stop-gates. Later Gilbert lowered the sill of the sea-gates by five inches and moved them two hundred yards nearer to the estuary.[58] The fall in the sluice was altered, so that in some places the sluice was twenty feet deep. By 1783 the work had reached the mere and in five days the head of water drained away. A hundred miles of ditches were then dug around the new fields using a draining or guttering plough drawn by eight and sometimes ten horses at the rate of eight miles a day.

The results of all this work were phenomenal. By 1784 some of the land was dry enough to plough and yielded spring corn while the rest could be used for pasture on which Thomas Eccleston fattened Scotch cattle. In order to maintain the ditches, Eccleston made orders through his court leet. For instance, in 1788 it was specified that the old mill brook had to be two and a half yards wide from the old mill to Bescar meadow and at least three yards wide from there to Martin Mere. The boundary ditch was to be two yards wide and at least two feet deep. If the tenants of the land alongside those watercourses did not maintain them at the specified width and depth, they were brought before the court leet and fined. One complaint made in 1789 names William Culshaw, Thomas Burrows, James Whalley, James Charnock, James Turton, James Bond and John Sephton and records that they were all fined 'for neglecting to effectively deepen, widen and open their respective shares in the brook from the old mill'.[59]

Unfortunately in 1789 the Leeds and Liverpool canal burst its banks and flooded the reclaimed land once again, this time from the opposite direction. The drainage through the sluice successfully cleared the flood, but after the disaster, Thomas Eccleston decided to use the ground as pasture, rather than risk another flood spoiling the crops. For his achievement in successfully draining a great part of the mere, Thomas Eccleston was awarded the gold medal of the Society of Arts, Manufactures and Commerce.

In 1809 a high tide swept away both the sea-gates and the flushing gates, but the stop-gates held and prevented another disaster. Later it was decided to substitute cast iron cylinders with valves for the original gates, but these were no better and became silted up before very long, and the floods again took over. It was not until 1849 that an efficient method of pumping the water away using steam pumps, was introduced in the north-eastern section of the mere by Sir Thomas Dalrymple Hesketh of Rufford. Not long after, the Scarisbrick trustees installed a similar system at Crossens at the cost of £60,000, and since then the mere has gradually been reduced in size and more of the fertile black earth has been reclaimed.

In the 1950s a modern pumping system was introduced and after that the farmers on the reclaimed mosslands in Scarisbrick could at last plant their seeds in the spring with the confidence that they would reap their crops in the autumn. Before this later improvement, many tenant

6. A view of the flooded mosslands of Scarisbrick during the winter of 1995.

farmers suffered heavy losses and were even forced to leave their holdings as a result of flooding and repeated crop failure. Now all those
difficulties are put on one side – if not forgotten – and this extremely
fertile soil yields several kinds of grain and all kinds of vegetables for
the market. Nevertheless, in the winter-time after severe rains it is often
possible to see the mere spreading water logged fingers out again over
its former territory, especially where it used to flow into the river
Douglas.

Jacobitism

While the Scarisbricks and their tenants were busy improving their
lands, the Jacobite movement was causing anxiety to the authorities.
Everyone was under suspicion, especially the Catholics who were suspected of supporting the exiled Catholic King James II and of plotting
to restore him to the throne. There is little evidence to link the Scarisbrick family with any real Jacobite activity, but it is undeniable that
they had family connections with some of the plotters. A distant relative,
William Dicconson from Wrightington was accused of being one of
those involved in the Lancashire plot of 1694. Although he was acquitted, he later fled to France and joined the court at St Germain, where
he became under-governor to James, Prince of Wales, and later treasurer
to Mary of Modena, widow of James II.

Robert Scarisbrick was suspected of being involved in the rising of
1715. Definitely he had been in hiding with two other suspects, John
Ashton and John Gregson, and when the Act of Clemency was passed
in 1717, they surrendered to Lord Chief Justice Parker. The Scarisbrick
estates were confiscated and Robert was committed to Newgate prison,
where Nicholas Blundell and his wife visited him. Eventually Robert
was allowed bail and went for trial at Lancaster Assizes in March 1718.
He was acquitted and his estates were restored to him.[60]

The Standish family, friends of the Scarisbricks, were also implicated
in the plot of 1694, and although they too were acquitted at that time,
later letters from Mrs Standish preserved among the Scarisbrick archives
indicate that she supported the Stuart cause. These bring news of the
progress of Jacobite forces in 1745 and of the destruction of the Warring-
ton bridge to deter the rebels. Another interesting document which

leaves no doubt as to where the sympathies of the Scarisbrick family lay, was found among their papers. It is a Jacobite song, ostensibly a shepherd's song;

> Heaven bless our old Landlord and send him again
> Ere famine and poverty kill the poor swain
> Ere the Dutch all our wealth and our honours do reap
> And fleece this poor nation as I fleece my poor Sheep.

Of course, Jacobite activity was necessarily clandestine, and so evidence of it is extremely hard to find. Nevertheless, to piece together all the clues would be a very rewarding piece of research for a historian. It might also be possible to discover whether the sympathies of the lord of the manor permeated down to his tenantry, but time does not permit me such a detailed study at the moment.

CHAPTER 2

RELIGION IN SCARISBRICK

The Catholics

 S WE HAVE READ, Scarisbrick was one of the six townships comprising the parish of Ormskirk from very early times. It is not known exactly when the first church in Ormskirk was founded, but it was evidently in existence before Burscough priory was built, because in the foundation charter for the priory (1189), Robert son of Henry of Latham, granted Ormskirk church together with some other properties to the Austin or Black canons as a source of income for the new priory. Built into the eastern wall of the church is a remnant of a stone cross shaft, possibly dating from Saxon times, and it is thought by some archaeologists that the stone was part of a preaching cross which predated the church, but until the stone can be removed from the eastern wall, it is difficult to be more definite about its origin. Nevertheless, it is certain that Ormskirk was a centre of Christianity long before the Norman Conquest.

The bases of several stone crosses have been found within the township of Scarisbrick. Although these may have been purely devotional crosses or roadside shrines, it is more likely that they were burial crosses judging by their positions. Until the last century, coffins were carried by relatives of the deceased to the funeral, and when the church was some distance away, the bearers needed to rest their load. Consequently crosses were erected to mark suitable resting places where the mourners could gather, offer prayers for the dead and either change the bearers or, if no others were available, give them an opportunity to rest.

In the immediate area around Scarisbrick the remains of eighteen crosses were recorded on early maps or were mentioned in charters or deeds, some dating from as early as the thirteenth century. These crosses marked two routes across the township: one to Burscough Priory following a pathway to the north of the Hall and the other to Ormskirk following the course of the present-day Southport road. The most westerly cross in the township was at Carr Cross and to the east of

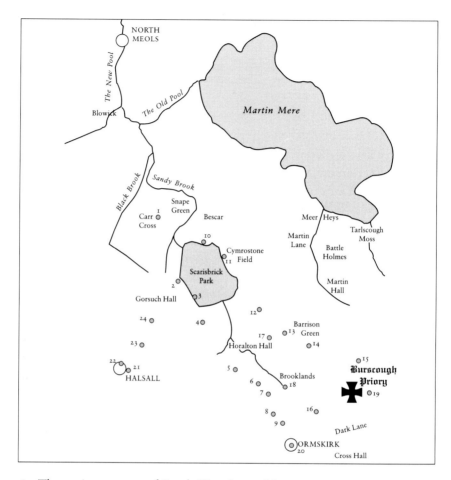

6a. The ancient crosses of South West Lancashire.

1. Carr Cross	13. Barrison Green Cross
2. Gorsuch Cross	14. Throstle's Nest Cross
3. Scarisbrick Park Cross	15. Pippin Street Cross
4. Pinfold Cross	16. Bath Wood Cross
5. Harleton Gate Cross	17. Moorfield Lane Cross
6. Wood End Cross	18. Brooklands Cross
7. Heskin Hall Cross	19. Burscough Priory Cross
8. Hales Cross	20. Ormskirk Cross
9. Stock Bridge Cross	21. Halsall Churchyard Cross
10. Bescar Brow Cross	22. Halsall Village Cross
11. Cliffe Wood Cross	23. North Moor Cross
12. Turton's Cross	24. Morris Lane Cross

The large circles indicate Pre-Reformation Churches
Adapted from H. Taylor, *Ancient Crosses and Holy Wells of Lancashire* (Manchester: Sherratt & Hughes 1906), p. 121

that cross, the two routes diverged. The one to Burscough was marked by crosses at Bescar Brow, Clyffe Wood, Turton's Cross – at the roadside between Hurleston and Barrison Green Lane, Barrison Green – at the crossing between Barrison Green Lane and Moorfield Lane and one at Throstle's Nest, Pippin Street, outside the present Scarisbrick boundary. The road to Ormskirk was marked by crosses at Gorsuch, Scarisbrick Hall, Pinfold, Hurleston and five others outside the township boundary; at Wood End (Blindman's Lane), Heskin Hall, Hales, Brooklands (Narrow Moss Lane) and Stock Bridge. The exact location of these crosses can be seen on the accompanying map. They seem to have been spaced at intervals of one third of a mile and if this was the original plan, two sites remain unidentified between Pinfold and Hurleston.

Throughout the country many of the bases of burial crosses were still in place as late as the nineteenth century, and the custom of stopping the funeral procession at crosses was continued, but now few can be found and the custom has been abandoned. In this township only the cross within the grounds of Scarisbrick Hall has been preserved. It has been described as a vinegar cross, possibly on account of the medieval and Tudor custom of anointing the mourners with vinegar, stored in a recess in the crosses, as a precaution against the spread of infection, especially in times of plague.

Another version of the origin of the vinegar crosses was that in times of plague, food was left at the crosses to be collected by the plague victims. They left the money to pay for their provisions in a bowl of vinegar to prevent any infection passing to the tradesmen. The victims of the plague were isolated in cabins erected some distance away from the homes of the townsfolk in order to prevent the spread of the infection, before the plague finally receded in the late seventeenth century. It is possible that the fields named on the tithe map of 1839, as 'Cabin Hey' mark the location of these plague cabins. Two were to the west of Southport Road, opposite to the site of the isolation hospital of New Hall, while the others, north of Couplands near the site of the railway line, possibly served the eastern side of the township.

There are holes in the shaft of the Scarisbrick cross, but they seem to have been made to secure a carved timber crucifix on the face of the cross, rather than to form an alcove for a bowl of vinegar. Nearby is a well where the thirsty bearers would have drunk before proceeding

on their journey to Ormskirk. Before the wall was built around the
Hall grounds, there was an open place – similar to a present-day lay-by –
beside the roadway, where mourners could gather around the cross.
Later, when the road was widened all that remained was the present
small enclosure around the cross.

The medieval lords of the manor and early members of the Scarisbrick
family were buried in the priory. However, before the Reformation that
custom was abandoned. The will of Thomas Scarisbrick dated 1530
confirms that by that date deceased members of the family were taken
to Ormskirk Church for burial. During alterations to the church 1877–
91, a large brass depicting a member of the family was found under
the floor of the Scarisbrick chapel. It was probably a memorial to Henry
who married Katherine, daughter of Sir John Pilkington and who later
fought at the battle of Agincourt. He survived the battle, but was killed
four years later in France at the siege of Sens. The surcoat on the brass
is similar to that worn by the king at Agincourt, and bears the arms
of Scarisbrick.[1] It is possible that this memorial was moved from Burscough Priory, or it may have been placed originally in Ormskirk
Church, and had been lost during one of the building's many alterations.
When the earth floor of the church was used as a graveyard, an old
memorial could easily be covered over and forgotten – especially when
the family commemorated did not attend the church regularly.

The distance between Ormskirk and Scarisbrick made it difficult for
the elderly and the infirm to attend mass in the parish church, and so
one of the priests from Ormskirk or Burscough used to ride to the
township and say mass at pre-arranged locations. The first reference
to these local services dates from 1430 when Jane Scarisbrick obtained
permission from the Bishop of Lichfield and Coventry to hold 'divine
services in a low voice' in her home. Some years later the Scarisbrick
family either built or converted part of their property into a chapel for
the use of their family, servants, friends and tenantry, and in 1447 this
chapel in the Hall, the first one recorded in Scarisbrick, was licensed
by the bishop.

The Reformation brought a great split in the religious allegiance of
the townsfolk of Scarisbrick. Some followed the guidance of Henry VIII
and converted to Protestantism, but many – including the lord of the
manor – maintained their loyalty to the old faith, Catholicism. This
was against the law, and so mass had to be said secretly by priests

whose identity and place of residence were also closely guarded secrets. Consequently it is extremely difficult to trace exactly what happened to the chapel of 1447 and its congregation over the following two hundred years. Certainly immediately before the Reformation, the chapel within the Hall was listed in the will of Thomas Scarisbrick dated 1530, where the inventory included 'two vestments, two chasubles, two albs, a chalice, two mass-books, twelve images closed in box cases, and two not closed, and various altar linen'.[2] At that time the chapel would still be served by priests centred at Ormskirk or Burscough, who travelled around the district performing various religious duties. Then fifty years later, after the dissolution of the monasteries, Humphrey Cartwright joined the Scarisbrick household on his return from Douai, and conducted services in the chapel in the Hall. As we will see in the following chapter, this Benedictine monk also taught in the village.

English Catholics who refused to attend the parish church or who refused to take the Oath of Supremacy accepting the monarch as the head of the English Church, were described as recusants and were liable to pay heavy fines. The lords of the manor of Scarisbrick gave the impression that they were conforming by practising the Protestant faith to avoid confrontation with the authorities. For instance, during the reign of Elizabeth, Edward Scarisbrick served as a justice of the peace, an office which could officially only be held by a Protestant. He was described by a contemporary as 'conformable', and yet it was known that his wife and daughters followed the Catholic faith – as he undoubtedly did in secret.

In July 1626 the government adopted a law permitting Catholics to compound and many landowners chose to take advantage of the scheme. This meant that instead of continually paying recusancy fines, they contracted to pay an annual rent based on the assessed value of 66 per cent of their landed property. Technically once a Catholic had compounded, he was no longer liable for recusancy fines. The aim of the government in adopting this measure was to raise a continual supply of money without ruining the source of supply. Of course, many ways were found of concealing the true value of the landed estates. Some estates were divided or entailed to the next generation and others were transferred to Protestant friends. The Scarisbrick family drew up an indenture on 29 March 1630, conveying part of the estate to the wife of Edward Scarisbrick for life, while the rest remained in Edward's hands also for life.[3]

Charles I disbanded Parliament when Sir John Bankes was Attorney General (1634–40). Consequently, the king could not appeal to Parliament for financial help, even though he was extremely short of funds. Their solution to the problem was to instruct the justices to apply the penal laws more stringently in order to produce more money for Charles I. Edward Scarisbrick was one of the victims of this situation. He was convicted on 20 August 1635 and accused of repeated violations of the penal code. All his property was seized by the Crown for life, so the rents were then paid to the Crown. If the 1630 indenture had not been made, the Crown may have seized all his land and offered it for sale, but as he only held the property for life, that could not be done. He chose to compound for £16 6s. 8d. on 66 per cent of his land, but he still had to pay arrears in fines owing since his previous conviction in 1633. In 1640 the government reviewed his recusancy and inflicted even more penalties.[4] Despite all attempts to avoid their effects, the penal laws resulted in difficulties for Catholics of every income bracket.

The accounts of the constables of Scarisbrick (1666–67) list various expenses incurred as they applied the laws against recusants. They drew up warrants for their arrest and took lists of the guilty to Ormskirk Quarter Sessions. We do not know who exactly was involved at that time, but by 1679 the continual recusancy fines were having dire effects on certain of the poorer Catholics in the township. In fact, the church-wardens and overseers of the poor for Scarisbrick were so concerned about the poverty of some of the townsfolk accused of recusancy, that they appealed to the justices of the peace at the Quarter Sessions in Wigan to discharge certain Catholics from their recognisances. The document explains that these people were 'very poor and indigent . . . by reason of their being continued bound for recusancy from session to session' – each session they were bound over on payment of a set amount to appear at the next session – with the result that they were 'reduced to such a low and mean condition that in a very short time they must be chargeable and burdensome to the inhabitants of the parish of Ormskirk'. The list included Kathleen, Alice and John Spencer, Jane the wife of Thomas Blundell, Ellen Adamson, Alice and Edward Halsall, Ann Barton, Elizabeth Sutch, Cicely Norres, Henry and Oliver Titterington, Margery Lyon, Margaret Birch, Mary Peterson, Anne Low and James Worthington junior. John Entwistle, the lawyer, of Ormskirk attached his plea to that of the overseers, saying that he knew about the desperate situation of these people and asked the justices to discharge them. His plea succeeded and the recusants were excused from making any further payment.[5] It is significant that the justices were prepared to be lenient at this particular time, the year of the Popish plot of Titus Oates whereby he accused certain Catholics – including Edward Scarisbrick – of plotting against Charles II. This 'plot' resulted in a great wave of anti-Catholicism throughout the land. Evidently, the judges in this part of Lancashire were influenced more by feelings of compassion for their neighbours – or perhaps by concern about the possible large increase rise in the local poor rate – than by national opinions.

In order to avoid prosecution, the recusants evolved secret ways of communicating with other Catholics. In fact, Francis Scarisbrick SJ, son of Edward, went so far as to write the instructions for invisible writing in his notebook. If the powder of vitriol and water were used on paper, the writing could not be read unless the paper was dampened with water 'wherein the powder of gall has been infused'. Exactly what substance was meant by 'vitriol' at that date is not known, but it was some kind of acid. Sometimes Anglican friends were used as messengers, as for instance in 1701 when a warning to Robert Scarisbrick was sent by Lawyer Starkie in a letter from an Anglican clergyman. He warned Robert to go into Cheshire or Yorkshire or anywhere else out of the county to avoid an impending summons for recusancy.[6] Various kinds of subterfuge continued to be necessary for the Catholics until religious toleration was accepted officially after the First and Second Catholic Relief Acts of 1778 and 1791.

We know that the chapel in the Hall was still in use in 1608, for it was listed in the inventory of the goods of Henry Scarisbrick, but we do not know which priest ministered there at that time. However, from 1618 until 1774 a continuous line of priests – mainly Jesuits – who served at Scarisbrick, can be traced from the records kept by the continental houses, where the priests were trained for the English mission. They lived in the Hall and performed religious duties for the family and for neighbouring Catholics.

Priests serving Scarisbrick Chapel 1579–1825

1579–1582	Humphrey Cartwright OSB
1618–1635	Michael Alford SJ
1622–1640	Francis Thompson SJ
1641–1642	Cormac Fields
1642–1643	Bryan Cansfield SJ
1643–1648	Lawrence Sankey SJ
1637	Henry Howard
1648–1666	Ferdinand Poulton SJ
1666–1673	Peter Bradshaigh SJ
1674	Thomas Scarisbrick SJ
1674–1678	John Penketh SJ
1653–1680	Christopher Bradshaigh
1679–1688	Henry Scarisbrick SJ
1689–1693	John Malbon
1693	Thomas Blundell SJ
1698	Albert Bapthorpe SJ
1701–1708	John Smith SJ
1708–1716	John Maynard SJ
1716–1731	William Scarisbrick
1731–1747	Cornelius Murphy SJ
1754–1767	Thomas Conyers SJ
1735–1773	Nicholas Fouriers SJ
1771–1778	Edward Scarisbrick SJ
1774–1791	Robert Johnson SJ
1791–1792	John Hurst
1792–1802	Abbe Buchet
1802	John Kenyon OSB
1802–1825	Abbe Dorival

Several of these priests suffered as a result of their Catholic faith. Bryan Cansfield alias Christopher Benson SJ, 1642–43, lived at the Hall and travelled around the north of England as a Catholic missionary, saying Mass whenever he could gather a few fellow believers together. A Yorkshire judge whose wife had been converted to the Catholic faith by a Jesuit priest, mistakenly thought that Cansfield had been responsible for her conversion. He was so angry that he sent soldiers to arrest the priest, and Cansfield was seized at the altar, cruelly beaten and carried off to prison in York Castle, where he was beaten, kicked and starved. Later the judge found that he had accused the wrong Jesuit, but although he sent a quick reprieve, it was too late. Cansfield, then over sixty years of age, died in prison on 4 August 1645.[7] Another priest John Poulton, who served at Scarisbrick from 1648 until 1666, also died as a result of his ministry, but this time the priest died of the plague, which he caught while ministering to victims of the disease among his congregation.

After the death of James Scarisbrick in 1675, there was no mention of the chapel in his inventory, but, as I suggested in an earlier chapter, it could easily have been converted into a dining room when the assessors came to value the deceased's property. Certainly, that kind of subterfuge was necessary in the decade 1675–85 when there was a great increase in anti-Catholic feeling throughout the land. This upsurge in anti-popery was caused by widespread suspicion regarding the intentions of James, the brother of Charles II and heir to the throne, who was known to follow the Catholic faith. Rumours were circulated that Catholicism would again become the established faith of England, and that the future James II would allow the Pope to control the land. These suspicions surfaced in the conspiracy of Titus Oates and the Popish Plot, when Catholics were falsely accused of plotting against Charles II. Many Catholic gentry, particularly those in Lancashire where Catholicism was more widespread than in other parts of England, felt extremely vulnerable during these times of plots and counter-plots, and fled to France in the winter and spring of 1678–79.

A year before the death of James Scarisbrick, John Penketh SJ, 1674–78, accepted his appointment to Scarisbrick on condition that he was to be at liberty to 'make excursions into the neighbouring villages'.[8] Then, according to a contemporary source, 'he passed his time with the humbler class of society and always made his rounds of the neighbourhood on foot'. Unfortunately, the anti-Catholic suspicions were directed particularly against the Jesuits, because many of them had been trained in France and so were thought to have the support of the French government. They were falsely accused of planning a French invasion in order to make the Catholic James, then Duke of York, king. One night when Father Penketh was travelling to a remote village under cover of darkness, he was intercepted by a justice of the peace and taken to Lancaster Gaol to await trial at the Assizes. At the trial evidence

was given against him by John Gorsuch, a local man who had studied
for the priesthood. Father Penketh was convicted of priesthood and
sentenced to be hanged, drawn and quartered. His many friends and
supporters petitioned for his reprieve and eventually this was granted.
Nevertheless, he was confined for six years in a tiny cell with very little
food and no fire even in the depth of winter. After the trial Gorsuch
was ostracised by the Catholic community.[9]

Several of the younger sons of the Scarisbrick family trained abroad
and returned to serve their own family and tenantry in secret. Henry,
1679–88, came home to Scarisbrick soon after the imprisonment of Father Penketh, and was ministering in the district in 1688 when
William III landed in England and James II's queen, Mary (of Modena),
fled to France. The situation for Catholics was again so menacing that
Henry felt it was wiser to flee to the continent in order to avoid any
backlash against Catholics after the coronation of the Protestant William III. During the early years of the eighteenth century, many Catholics
were imprisoned for their faith and John Maynard, the Jesuit in residence at the Hall from 1708 until 1716, used to travel to Chester to
minister to the prisoners in the castle – possibly some of them were
Catholics from Scarisbrick.

Unfortunately, while he was there, he caught an infectious disease
and died. After this tragedy, another member of the Scarisbrick family,
Edward SJ moved back into the Hall, and served as a priest in the
district between 1716 and 1731. He was a friend of the Catholic,
Nicholas Blundell of Crosby and frequently dined with him.

In 1732, Robert Scarisbrick, then lord of the manor and also great
friend of Nicholas Blundell, made notes around the margins of a book,
A Missive of Consolation (Louvain 1647) as we have seen.[10] Besides
recording births, marriages and deaths in the township, he also noted
all kinds of day-to-day matters. Among these notes was one – 'the seats
in ye chapel maide with green cittermister, November 24th 1732'. This
entry confirms that the chapel was definitely in use at that date and
suggests that the previous seats had been worn out with constant use
and had been replaced by ones in green Kidderminster carpeting.

Gradually, as religious toleration spread, priests who had relied for
over two hundred years on the protection and generosity of their
'country-house' patrons, were able to emerge from the shadows and
abandon their lives of secrecy. In many cases, their position in the halls

had placed an intolerable burden upon them because their patrons expected obedience and subservience from them. For instance, in 1707 Nicholas Blundell, the patron of a priest in Little Crosby, complained to the provincial of the Jesuits in the area about the behaviour of the Crosby priest, Father Polyntz. An enquiry was conducted and the priest was moved. Then Nicholas sent a letter to the Provincial listing all the qualities he expected in the next priest to be appointed.[11]

Whether the Scarisbrick family had adopted a similar attitude to their priests is not known, but certainly Robert Johnson SJ (1774–91) preferred his independence, and moved into Lime Kiln House near Heaton's Bridge.[12] There he supported himself with the help of the rents from the Priest's Farm on Martin Lane. Of course there may have been a different explanation for his move, for at that time another member of the family, Edward SJ, who was an invalid, had returned and ministered at the little chapel in the Hall between 1771 and 1778. Perhaps the two priests had arranged to divide the mission between them, one serving in the Hall and one in the village, but it is significant that the priest did not return to live in the Hall when Edward died in 1778.

Eventually in 1778, when the Catholic Relief Act was passed, the celebration of mass became legal and the need to conceal the existence of the chapel had passed. As the population of Scarisbrick increased in the late eighteenth century, and more Catholics attended services, it became very difficult for the congregation to worship in the tiny chapel which was only thirty feet long by twenty feet wide. The 1767 returns of the Papists gives us some idea of the problem. This listing gives the name, age, occupation and birthplace of all Catholics in each township in the parish of Ormskirk. Altogether 247 people were listed in Scarisbrick. As most of these would attend mass whenever possible, the tiny chapel must indeed, have been very overcrowded. Admittedly the family worshipped in an ante-room, but it is known that sometimes the worshippers were compelled to hear Mass from the landing outside the room or even on the staircase leading up to it. The move to a larger church was long overdue.

Towards the end of the eighteenth century, religious toleration spread and the harassing of Catholics on account of their beliefs, ceased. Finally, in 1791 Parliament accepted this alteration in the national attitude towards Catholics, and granted them the right to build and use licensed chapels.[13] However, in France conditions were rapidly deteriorating following the French Revolution and Catholic priests were subject to great hostility. Consequently many were forced to flee to England and find positions in this country. Two of these, Abbé Buchet, 1792–1802, and Abbé Dorival, 1802–24, accepted the hospitality of the Scarisbrick family, took up residence at the Hall and ministered to the Catholics of Scarisbrick.

However, in 1809 Thomas Eccleston, who inherited the estate and changed his name to Scarisbrick, decided to improve the Tudor hall. Some parts were to be demolished and others were to be encased in brick. During these building operations Abbé Dorival moved out of the Hall into the township and the small chapel within the hall was demolished. To replace it, the tithe barn adjoining the site of the present St Elizabeth's was bought and converted into a chapel. A cross was mounted on the eastern end of the roof, windows were inserted along each side, and in 1812 the Church of St Mary was opened. Although this was a very plain chapel, most Catholic churches were very simple at this time. After centuries of persecution the Catholics preferred to keep a low profile and indeed the Act of 1791 specified that they were allowed to build chapels – not churches – without steeples or bells. When the French Abbé Dorival died in 1826 the Benedictine order at Douai Abbey near Woolhampton, accepted the mission and began their tradition of ministering to the Scarisbrick Catholics.

The new chapel proved to be so successful, that in 1846 Charles Scarisbrick, the squire, decided to enlarge it. Five large windows were put along each side of the extended building and a bell in a frame was erected on the western end of chapel roof. At the same time two acres of land were bought and some time later, the present presbytery was built.

Benedictine monks serving in Scarisbrick 1826–

1826	Augustine Shann
1826–1865	Joseph Benedict Hoole
1865	Richard Birchall
1865–1870	Peter Ignatus Greenough
1870–1873	John Placid Hall
1873–1882	W. Bulbeck
1882–1884	John Hall
1884–1887	E. D. Ross

1887–1898	James Rowley
1897–1912	James Furniss
1912–1913	Anthony Jordan
1913–1918	Gilbert Atherton
1919–1925	Francis O'Shaughnessy
1925–1955	Cuthbert Griffin
1955–1965	Bruno Teeley
1965–1970	Mark Ackers
1970–1971	J. A. Eckersley
1971–1991	Philip Robinson OSB
1991–1992	James Donovan
1992–	Leo Arkwright

The next great change came in 1889 when the present church of St Elizabeth was opened. It was built at the joint expense of the Marquis, and his son and daughter-in-law, the Count and Countess de Casteja and was dedicated to St Elizabeth in memory of Lady Elizabeth who died in 1872. The family chose the firm of Pugin and Pugin to be architects for the project and so continued the association begun when Augustus Welby Pugin designed the major part of their Victorian Hall. The style of architecture echoes the Gothic style of the Hall, and within the church are many reminders of the family's close connection with the continent. The altar is constructed of stone from Caen in Normandy, the stations of the cross were enamelled on zinc by Maillart of Paris and the pulpit – thought to have been carved in the sixteenth century – originated in either Holland or Belgium. The stained glass windows in the sanctuary are examples of English craftsmanship and were designed by Hardman of Birmingham. The one in the centre featuring St Elizabeth at the Visitation was presented by local Catholics. The old barn church of St Mary provided the first bell for St Elizabeth's, and it hung in a turret over the chancel arch. When the church was newly built, the Casteja family had their own chantry chapel within the building, and could enter it through a private entrance which led directly into their grounds.

Many Catholic dignitaries gathered on 28 April 1889 for the opening of the Church, which was decorated with masses of flowers for the occasion. Music was provided by choristers from St Mary's in Wigan accompanied by an orchestra also from Wigan. During the offertory

7. The new church of St Elizabeth alongside the old church of St Mary in 1889.

8. The elaborately carved pulpit in St Elizabeth's church. It was part of the Marquis's collection of carvings, and when it was donated to the church, it had to be reduced in size.

the 'Ave Maria' was sung by Mrs Foster while Mr McEleny played the accompaniment on a clarinet. Originally it had been intended not to have an collection, but the congregation had expressed the wish to contribute towards the cost of both the window and an organ for the church. Altogether £400 was donated – a considerable amount for those days. In his address Monsignor Carr drew a parallel between the building of the temple by Solomon and the building of St Elizabeth's. He referred to the lord of the manor as the father, protector and guardian of his tenantry, and stressed that it was the duty of the local Catholics to reciprocate by maintaining the church in gratitude to the family for their generosity in erecting such a splendid place of worship for the use of their tenantry.

The Scarisbrick family continued to make additions to St Elizabeth's.

9. The interior of St Elizabeth's showing the Gothic style of its architecture.

10. A procession at St Elizabeth's in the 1950s. *Left to right*: Kenneth Whalley, John Charnock, Father Griffin, George Porter, Margaret Kershaw, Philomena Olverson, Winnie Church, Jack Charnock.

11. The May Queen at St Elizabeth's, taken in front of Church House. Pat Critchley, Christine Lea, Edwin Johnson, Dorothy Bradshaw, Josephine Charnock, Doreen Lydiate, Phyllis Charnock, Janet Huyton.

In 1898 they donated a 9.5 cwt bell cast by Charles Carr of Smethwich, in honour of the marriage of Count Andrea. The Bishop of Liverpool blessed the bell and it was named Pauline after the young bride. On this bell, which is still used today, is the inscription 'I summon the faithful, I mourn the dead, I give praise to God'. Then, after the Great War, the Marquis gave his family's chantry chapel to the church to be converted into a Lady Chapel in memory of those parishioners – including his own son, Count Emmanuel – who lost their lives in the war. Money already collected towards a war memorial by the local priest, Father O'Shaunessy, was used to make the necessary alterations to the church, and the Dowager Marchioness presented a group of the Madonna and Child by Luccia della Robbia, to enhance the chapel. The Scarisbrick family also endowed St Elizabeth's with an annuity of £100 per annum, but unfortunately that was lost many years later when the family had monetary problems.

Nowadays the church stands as a memorial to the family's great generosity, but the upkeep of such a unique building is a heavy responsibility for the local Catholic congregation. The priests still come from the Benedictine community centred at Douai, where there is continual support for the mission at Scarisbrick. A constant reminder of this close connection with the abbey are the present wrought iron entrance gates to the grounds of the church, where the arms of the abbey are an integral part of the design.

The Protestants

Those who abandoned the Catholic faith at the Reformation continued to worship at Ormskirk church. In those days it was a much smaller church than it is now, and its earthen floor was covered in places with tombstone slabs over the graves of the many families, who held the right to be buried within the church. It was the custom for these families to erect seats over the graves for use during the long services.

One of these privileged families was the Hurlestons of Hurleston Hall. They arranged for a door to be put across the entrance to their pew and had the name JOHN HURLESTON 1618 carved upon it, and whenever they were not using the pew, this door was locked. However, they moved away from the district and leased their manor house to

Richard Halsall, the Earl of Derby's solicitor. As the tenant of the Hall, he had the right to use the pew together with his family and servants. As this pew was adjacent to that of the Earl of Derby, it was very attractive to those who wanted to see and to be seen in the church.

However, in 1634 when Laud was Archbishop of Canterbury, an order was made that all churches in England were to be made more fitting for the worship of God. All the pews were to be made 'uniform' – alike – and were all to face in same direction. Consequently the old pew was removed to Hurleston Hall, where it was used as a settle for many years. The church authorities paid for benches with back rails to be made and erected in the church, and the body of the church was divided into four quarters for the use of the parishioners living in different parts of the parish. Thus all the tenants of Scarisbrick were expected to sit in the block of benches provided for their part of the parish. The congregation found these benches cold and draughty after the comfort of their own boxed-in pews, so gradually 'for warm's sake and to keep the wind and cold from their backs and legs' various families, including the Halsalls, put wainscoting 'betwixt their benches and the back rail and under the benches' converting them into pews as we know them.[14] Later William Halsall, the son of Richard, moved away from Scarisbrick and the manor house was let to tenants who did not frequent the church. However, many years later in 1672 John Hurleston, now of Pickton in Cheshire, applied for the right to renew his family's ancient privilege and to enclose a pew for the exclusive use of his household. The parishioners organised a petition opposing the granting of the right, because there was a great shortage of seats in the church at that time and it was felt that even when the pews were owned by individuals, they should be left open for anyone to use if necessary, especially when the owner was not a resident in the area. Evidently elitism in the church was unpopular amongst the parishioners of Ormskirk.

Several of the early vicars of Ormskirk were puritan, preferring a simple service with few, if any, vestments. Indeed one, John Broxxop, was accused of not wearing his surplice for the services in 1633 and was brought before the Bishop's court in Chester. The Puritans realised that there was a need for a chapel on the western boundary of the parish of Ormskirk and shortly after the Civil War, one was opened in Scarisbrick to which Mr Gawin Barkley, 'an able orthodox and godly preaching minister' was appointed. He was paid £50 by the State by an order from the Honourable Committee of Plundered Ministers. This committee, constituted by the Puritans, intended that a parish should be formed around this chapel in Fleet Street (the area around Southport Rd, near the Morris Dancers). We do not know the exact location of this early chapel, but as we will see in the next chapter, the old grammar school was built in 1648 near Fleet Street, a short distance along Bescar Brow Lane, and it is possible that the chapel was in the same premises. However, with the restoration of Charles II all plans of creating a new parish were abandoned and Scarisbrick was returned to the care of the vicar of Ormskirk for another two hundred years.[15]

Nathaniel Heywood who became vicar in 1656, also held puritan beliefs and in 1662 after the restoration of Charles II, he was ejected from his position for refusing to comply to the Act of Uniformity. Although he could no longer hold services in Ormskirk church, he continued to preach and teach, travelling around the area. His biographer reported that 'in times of great danger, he hath preached at one house at the beginning of the night and then gone two miles a-foot over the mosses and preached towards morning to another company at another house' . . . 'nor was he scant and short in his sermons, but usually very long, two hours at least often three . . . his heart was so fully set upon his Master's work that he forgot his own strength and his hearers' patience'. In 1672 when the Presbyterians, as the ejected ministers and their followers were called, were allowed to register their meeting houses, Heywood registered two chapels; one in Bickerstaffe two miles south of Ormskirk and one in Scarisbrick three miles north of the parish church. The exact location of this 1672 chapel is again uncertain, but it is possible that it was the same chapel in Fleet Street founded in the 1640s, possibly in the old grammar school. Certainly, as the former vicar of the parish, Nathaniel Heywood may have remained a trustee of the school and so could have arranged to use the school on Sundays when it was not in use as a school. That would explain why it became known later as the Chapel School. Heywood attracted a good congregation in Scarisbrick and wrote to his brother 'I bless God my congregation is numerous and attentive' and added 'Oh that they were as fruitful!'. Exactly what he meant by that remark we will never know.

Shortly afterwards the licenses were revoked, but Heywood continued preaching regardless. He opposed the Catholic religion and according to his biographer was 'a notable Champion against the Papists'. There was a great rivalry between Heywood and the priest; in fact they could be described as friendly enemies. On one occasion when both had been visiting the same dying man, the priest was 'so vexed that he could not prevail with the party, that he writ queries for Mr Heywood to answer'. We do not know the outcome of this encounter, but Heywood continued to 'preach against the Popish Party in Scarisbrick'. He certainly had plenty of courage to preach against the faith of the Scarisbrick family within the bounds of their manor.

Finally in 1674 Heywood was taken to Wigan Quarter Sessions accused of preaching within five miles of his former church. After many of his influential friends had intervened on his behalf, he was allowed to return home until the next Sessions. When he appeared a month later, again supported by many friends including Lady Stanley from Bickerstaffe, his case was dismissed. He died in 1677 and his son, also Nathaniel, continued his ministry. By that time religious toleration was beginning to spread and in 1689 the Act of Toleration was passed allowing presbyterians to preach in licensed chapels throughout England. No doubt, the ministers of Ormskirk Presbyterian church would continue to take services at Scarisbrick during the eighteenth century, but few records remain of their work.

Meanwhile those who remained true to the Established Church continued to worship in the parish church at Ormskirk. The long journey, especially from the farms and cottages on the northern and western boundaries of Scarisbrick township, must have very demanding in the days when the roads were mainly rough tracks across open mossland, and the drainage system for the mosses was unreliable. Then, once the parishioners arrived at the church, they often had great difficulties finding seats. In fact in 1722 Bishop Gaskell of Chester commented after visiting Ormskirk that the church would not hold over six hundred people, and yet the township of Ormskirk alone had an estimated population of a thousand.[16] That did not include all the parishioners from Bickerstaffe, Burscough, Lathom, Skelmersdale and Scarisbrick who were also expected to attend that church. After the bishop had complained to the vicar and churchwardens, plans were made to enlarge the church, and by 1734 the building was completed. Galleries had been erected around the southern and western sides and seats had been provided 'for such as stand in need and will purchase the same at reasonable rates'.[17] Thirty years later the north aisle was extended and yet another gallery was added. At last there was enough seating to cater for all the parishioners.

St Mark's Church

Nevertheless, the problem of the journey remained and it was not until the 1850s that any attempt was made to solve it. The plight of his parishioners in Scarisbrick troubled the vicar of Ormskirk (1846–1850), the Reverend E. J. G. Hornby, so he introduced a scheme and a fund to build a church in the township. Charles Scarisbrick offered to give him a site for the new church and contributions poured into the fund. One society, the Incorporated Society for Promoting Enlargement and Building of Churches and Chapels, donated £100 to the fund on condition that 294 free seats were provided for 'the poorer inhabitants of this parish for ever', while another society catering especially for the diocese of Chester made a similar grant. By November 1851 the church was built 'finished, furnished and adorned',[18] and was licensed for the celebration of Divine Worship. By this time the Reverend Hornby had moved to another diocese and the work had been completed by his successor the Reverend William Edward Rawstone. However, it was not until 19 April 1853 that the church and burial ground were officially consecrated by the Bishop of Chester. The impressive ceremony was attended by all the neighbouring clergy, who heard the Bishop preach a sermon on charity based on I Corinthians, Chapter 13, using as his examples the generous benefactors of the new church.

Regular services at St Mark's were conducted by the Reverend Steadman, a perpetual curate responsible to the vicar of Ormskirk, because Scarisbrick remained an outpost of that parish. However, on 14 December 1869 Scarisbrick was made an independent parish, and the Reverend W. R. Ramsden became its first vicar. Nine years later the Marquis and Marchioness gave more land to St Marks to enlarge the churchyard and to provide a site for the school (see Chapter 3).

Since that day the loyal congregation has striven to improve and decorate their much-loved church. The church was enlarged with the addition of a vestry in 1908. The organ was moved into the old vestry, three new arches were opened into the body of the church, the positions of the pulpit and choir stalls were altered, and the chancel floor was raised and re-tiled. Then in 1947 William Freeman donated an electric organ to replace the original hand-operated one which had been pumped for many years by Gordon Chippendale. During the closing years of New Hall hospital, one of the patients embroidered a beautiful tapestry which she donated to the church and which now hangs on the balcony. More recently, between 1988 and 1990, several of the parishioners have made over two hundred kneelers for the congregation. These have various themes; some act as memorials, some depict scenes in Scarisbrick and others record events of note. When they were finally made up, some of the kneelers were converted into time capsules containing newspapers and other memorabilia relative to the late 1980s. The local branch of the Women's Institute undertook a similar task when they made a wall-hanging showing scenes in Scarisbrick to commemorate the centenary of the civil parish for the Scarisbrick village hall. Future historians will have no difficulty researching Scarisbrick of the twentieth century, for the parishioners of Scarisbrick have already portrayed it in a very tangible form.

12. The first vicar of Scarisbrick, the Reverend W. R. Ramsden (died 1909) and his wife outside St Mark's church.

13. The interior of St Mark's church.

On 6 June 1986 St Mark's parish hall was opened and dedicated by Bishop Flagg. At last the church's organisations had an independent meeting place, and functions could be held whenever it was most convenient, without having to consider the needs of the day school. It also provided facilities for the church to cater for the needs of the parishioners, when for instance luncheons were served to senior citizens – a welcome service which is still offered to the parishioners today.

The Good Shepherd Mission

The building of St Mark's Church did not solve the problems of many of the parishioners from the eastern part of the parish who still had a long way to travel to the services, and so in 1907 it was decided to erect a small mission at Hurleston Green. The Church authorities approached the Count de Casteja and he offered them land near Shaw Hall for a peppercorn rent on the condition that the land would be returned to the Scarisbrick estate, if the chapel ever ceased to be used.

Very few funds were available and it was thought that a corrugated iron building would be adequate for their needs. In the mid-1800s these 'tin chapels' were made in kit form by two firms in Liverpool; the

Windsor Iron Company and Francis Morton Ltd. Each joint was numbered so that the buyers could easily construct the chapel themselves, and consequently many small congregations bought these early examples of DIY and erected them in their own locality. They also had the advantage of being easy to re-assemble if there was a need to move the building. Enquiries were made around the district and eventually a suitable building which had once been used as a Seaman's Mission, was located in Wigan. It was easily disassembled, but then came the problem of how to get it to Scarisbrick. At last it was decided that, as the local farmers used the canal to transport their produce to Wigan market, the same barges could be used to carry the iron building back to Scarisbrick. This was agreed. The building was dismantled, floated down the canal, man-handled across the fields to the site and erected in its present position.

On 11 June 1907 the Good Shepherd Mission was dedicated by Bishop Chavasse of Liverpool. Among the local people present at the service were: Mr & Mrs Evan Heaton of Ball's Farm, Mr & Misses Heaton of Scarisbrick Bridge, Mr Thomas Berry of Scarisbrick House, Mr & Mrs George Sharrock of Hurlestone Hall, together with the new church-warden Mr Thomas Pilkington and sidesmen Mr James Moorcroft and Mr Philip Scarisbrick. After the formal part of the service, the Bishop read his licence of the room for the services of the Church of England

14. The Good Shepherd Mission.

15. The interior of the Good Shepherd Mission in 1955 with Mr Robert Alcock at the lectren.

16. Mr Vaughan.

17. Mr Samuel Price.

18. Mr George Thomas Hailwood.

19. A choir outing from the Mission and St Mark's. *Standing left to right*: ?, ?, Philip Scarisbrick, ?, ?, ?, ?, Hetty Scarisbrick?, ?, ?. *Seated*: Bob Livesey, Polly Livesey, Captain Holt, Alice Ackers, May Glover. *In front*: Lizzie Taylor, ?, ?.

20. The first Harvest Queen at the Good Shepherd Mission, 28 August 1848. *Back row*: Sheila Davey, Ethel Lloyd, Brenda Croston, Greta Baldwin. *Centre*: The Harvest Queen, Dorothy Scarisbrick. *Front row*: Leonard Wright, Marjorie Croston, Maureen Poole, Harry Hardman.

21. The Morris Dancers, 1949. *Back row*: Ethel Lloyd, Margaret Davey, Sheila Davey, June Snape, Margaret Wright, Mona Fletcher. *Second row*: Gillian Taylor, Mabel Lloyd, Maureen Ritchie, Brenda Howard, Jean Rigby. *Front row*: Norma Banks, Maureen Poole, Jane Merry.

and handed the document over to the Rev S. O. Bradley, vicar of Scarisbrick. The Bishop expressed the hope that the building which would hold 250 people, would cater for both the spiritual and social needs of the people of the district, and wished that every hamlet at any great distance from the parish church could have a similar building, which could be used for both religious purposes and social gatherings. He hoped that very soon the debt on the Mission, which cost £300, would be cleared and then the parishioners could enjoy the real benefits of their own mission room.

Through the years the Good Shepherd Mission has been served by several lay readers. The earliest was Mr Vaughan and he was followed by Samuel Price who lodged in Smithy Lane. Another servant of the Mission who deserves mention is Mr George Thomas Hailwood, who was both deaf and dumb, but nevertheless acted as bell ringer and verger at the Mission for many years. In the 1940's the first harvest queen, Dorothy Scarisbrick, was crowned and various functions including fancy dress parades and morris dancing displays, were organised to raise money to support the Mission. Although nowadays the Mission is seldom full to capacity, it is still served by a loyal band of parishioners.

Free Churches in Scarisbrick

One of the earliest of the nineteenth-century preachers who came to Scarisbrick, was Mr Greatbatch, a member of the Itinerant Society which at that time, was part of the Congregational Union. He shared a cottage with one of his 'hearers' in Newburgh, where he established a congregation of between sixty and seventy people in 1802. He travelled around the district gradually building up an extensive following, but although he visited Scarisbrick in 1807, it is not recorded that he had a regular congregation in the village.[19]

It was not until eighteen years later that a regular meeting of congregationalists was established by Mr Alexander of Churchtown who preached in a private house in Scarisbrick. Unfortunately, his host's family caught a fever and the meeting was forced to move out of doors. This was quite a usual venue for evangelical preachers, but although many were attracted and stayed to be converted, there were drawbacks in alfresco meetings. One experienced by Mr Alexander was that 'he was considerably annoyed in these labours by ill-disposed persons who did their utmost to disturb the congregation'.[20] He found it very difficult to maintain a regular following in the village, and virtually impossible to enlarge the congregation he had already attracted, because so many of the villagers were Roman Catholics. Finally at the end of the year when it was much too cold to preach outside, Mr Alexander abandoned his mission in Scarisbrick and moved to Banks.

Drummersdale Mission

A much more successful mission which is still thriving today, began in Scarisbrick in 1832. It was started by a member of the Congregational Church in Ormskirk, Richard Sephton, whose family farmed Bruff's farm in Drummersdale. He gathered a few children together in his father's kitchen and began teaching them each Sunday. The numbers increased until they needed a larger room. It was decided to convert the cart shed, but that needed funds which the tiny group could not afford. Nevertheless, they went ahead with the conversion. Later Richard told the story of how they found the money. He was out one day with his father looking at a small plot of land on which his father intended to sow corn. Richard suggested that it might produce good potatoes and his father offered to give him the proceeds of the crop if it succeeded. Richard accepted the offer and immediately set to work preparing the ground. The potatoes were planted and they grew so well that Richard's father said he had never seen potatoes produce such a very high yield. When the crop was sold it realised £21 10s., which Richard donated to the chapel. This amount together with the collection at the opening service paid all the cost of the building – not a shilling too little, nor a shilling too much. Some would say it was a miracle – combined with a lot of hard work. The Sunday school became so popular that when the scholars increased to over ninety children, they had to move some of the classes into the farmhouse.

Richard had many helpers and there is one amusing story about their methods and resourcefulness. One day Richard asked John Halsall, an uneducated man, to teach a class of boys. John protested that he could not read, but Richard insisted, 'Never mind, you'll get on', he said. One of the boys noticed that his teacher was holding his bible upside down to read. The boy pointed it out, only to get the reply, 'There's a sharp lad! Of course it's upside down'. As time went on John learned to read by teaching his charges the bible stories he knew by heart. There was a similar self-help attitude to the hymns. Richard had never been to Sunday school and so, did not know any of the tunes. Undaunted the little group made up a tune to 'Lord ascribe it to Thy grace . . .' from Watt's 'Divine Songs', and sang the same hymn every Sunday.

The group were so successful that Charles Scarisbrick heard about it and promised his support saying, 'If any one interferes with you let me know. And if you need a schoolroom, you shall have land and bricks to build one'. This was done and the small chapel now known affectionately as 'Dickies Mission' in Merscar Lane, was built.

Until 1922 the Mission operated as an independent evangelical mission served by lay preachers from Liverpool and Southport. Rev. Compton Smith of West End Congregational Church in Southport came

22. Inside Drummersdale Mission in 1963. *Back row*: Mr Wilfred Caunce, Mr Colin ?, Mr Richard Caunce (senior). *Third row*: Margaret Ollivier, Linda Westgate, ?, Joyce Neale, Linda Caunce, Shirley Ollivier, Mrs Winifred Caunce, Mrs Cicely Caunce, Mrs E. Powell. *Second row*: The Thomas sisters, ? Crompton, ?, ?. *Front row*: ?, Vivienne Ollivier, Roy Ollivier, (three brothers), Albert Sumner, (the Harrison brothers), Richard Caunce (junior).

23. The tip-up seats inside Drummersdale Mission with Mrs Elizabeth Peter and Mr Richard Caunce.

24. Extending Drummersdale Mission in 1975.

25. The Sunday School at Drummersdale Mission in 1956. *At the back*: Olive Madden and Mrs Rigby. Third row: Joyce Lawson, Margaret Caunce, ?, (Lawson sisters holding hands), (behind the little girl) Mary Caunce, Doris Rothwell, Alan Ashton, Nathan Baldwin, Brian Disley. *Second row*: Harold Neale, Mary Neale, Violet Culshaw, Phillip Caunce, John Robinson. *Front row*: ?, (visiting speaker), Elizabeth Neale, John Halsall, Nora Caunce, Wilfred Caunce.

to Scarisbrick periodically to give communion, and later in the 1880s Rev. A. S. Welch from Hawkshead St Church developed a close association with the mission. After Richard's death the responsibility for administering the chapel was taken over by his daughter. However as time passed, the work became too much for the ageing spinster and she tried to find some way of ensuring the mission's future. She enquired about the work of the Southport and District Christian Workers Association, which was responsible for Boundary St Mission in Southport and New Lane Mission in Burscough, and was very impressed. Consequently in 1922 after several meetings with the trustees, she transferred the responsibility of running the mission to them. Later the same year when the Marquis needed to realise his assets, they bought the property and an acre of ground from the Scarisbrick Estate for £100.

Gradually over the years, various improvements have been made to the property. In 1955 electricity replaced the old oil lamps. A coke central heating boiler was installed instead of the old coke stove which used to stand in the middle of the main hall, and now that has also been updated and a fully automated oil-fired boiler heats the whole building. A great innovation was made in 1970 when all the old wooden benches were removed and second-hand, re-upholstered, tip-up, cinema seats were installed and the whole main hall was carpeted. In 1975 the premises were enlarged to include a new kitchen and toilet facilities. That was a very welcome improvement for until that time, the toilets had been dry ones outside the building at the back of the church. Then in 1977 a new front entrance was built and shortly afterwards a modern car-park was added. The most recent alteration has been the double glazing of all the windows. Certainly, Dickie's Mission goes from strength to strength.

Wesleyan chapels

According to a directory of 1854,[21] the Wesleyans had two chapels in the township, one erected in 1843 and the other in 1849. I have been unable to trace the chapel built in 1843, but it is possible that the writer was referring to Drummersdale Mission. However, that was founded several years earlier and was not Wesleyan. Other candidates are New Lane chapel, Burscough – also not Wesleyan – and Halsall Methodist chapel but neither of these are within the bounds of the township, so the mystery remains.

The chapel which was founded in 1849 has been easier to trace. It was built on the site of the old pinfold as shown on the tithe map of 1839 at the corner of Pinfold Lane and Southport Rd, and according to the 1851 census William Smith aged 34, a Calvinistic minister from Radnor, and his wife Mary ministered at the chapel and also taught at a school there. By the time of the 1861 census the Smiths had moved on and their place had been taken by John Meredith aged 31, another Calvinistic Methodist minister and his wife Mary Ann. There is no record of any minister at Pinfold in the 1871 census, and both the chapel and the school seem to have been closed. In fact when the Countess bought the building at Pinfold to use as premises for the new school as required by the 1870 Education Act, it was described as 'formerly a Wesleyan chapel'. Part of the old chapel building is incorporated in the western part of present school. The window in the classroom overlooking Pinfold Lane has been altered, but as we can see, originally it was larger and rounded at the apex, a typical chapel window.

The Wesleyan Methodist Register of Baptisms for the period 1850–1870 records that five children were baptised at Scarisbrick: Lydia Blundell 19 August 1850, John Sumner 11 April 1853, Mary Caunce 11 April 1862, Ellen Molyneux 2 November 1864, and Sarah Williams 20 May 1866. These baptisms were performed by the superintendent minister of the Ormskirk circuit. Unfortunately the register does not record where in Scarisbrick the baptisms were performed, but it is likely that it was in the old Pinfold chapel.

Bescar Lane Methodist Church

Soon after the outbreak of the First World War, some young local preachers from Mornington Road Methodist Church were invited to Drummersdale Mission to take the services. They were very impressed by the success of the Mission and recognised the opportunity to found another free church in the area. At the next Quarterly Meeting of Mornington Road Chapel, they suggested that the Church should take the initiative to found another mission in Scarisbrick. The church members were very enthusiastic and formed a committee to organise a new Society in the village.

No premises were available for the services and so it was arranged to hold them in various private houses. Mrs Sykes, Mrs J. Seddon and Mrs J. Sephton offered their homes and all three were used regularly. Services were also frequently held in the open air, and the lusty hymn singing accompanied by an organ provided by some of the members of Boundary Street Mission in Southport, attracted people to these evangelical meetings. Each time a service was arranged, strong men in the congregation were enlisted to carry the organ to the appropriate place where it was played by Miss Elizabeth Thompson, who was the chapel organist in those early years. Members of the Southport Church loyally supported the new venture. They used to travel on the 5.10 p.m. train from Chapel Street to allow themselves time to call at some of the local houses, where they would invite people to join in their services. In return, the local members of the congregation would often provide the visitors with a meal before they caught their train back to Southport. Not long after the foundation of the group, it was decided to start a Sunday School at the home of Mrs Sykes at 14 Drummersdale Lane, and Mr Orphan, one of the original founding committee, became the first Sunday School Superintendent. In January 1916 they held their first tea-party and invited the Mayoress of Southport, Mrs Henry Ball, to join in the festivities. The scholars gave a musical entertainment and after tea they played all kinds of games until it was time to go home. Before they left each scholar was given a bag of fruit, nuts and chocolates. In later years the annual prizegiving was combined with the tea-party and it became the highlight of the scholars' year.

When Mrs Sykes left the district, the Sunday School was transferred to White House Farm, the home of Mrs Thompson and her family, and it was there, on 25 June 1916, that the first Sunday School Anniversary was held. Later that year the small community held their first Harvest Festival in this most appropriate setting. However, the congregation was expanding so rapidly that plans were made to build a church in Scarisbrick, and in the meanwhile, to buy two small cottages for their immediate need. These temporary premises in Woodmoss Lane were known as Wesley Hall and were opened on 27 March 1917 by the Chairman of the Liverpool District of Methodism, the Rev. I. Parker.

Methodists from the Southport churches gave their support to the plans for expansion and Southbank Church accepted the responsibility of overseeing the construction of the new church at the corner of Woodmoss Lane and Station Rd. Many fund-raising events were held including a sale of work which lasted three days and realised an amazing £2,000 for the project. At last on 15 September 1923, the twelve foundation stones of Bescar Lane Wesleyan Church were laid. It took less than a year to complete the building, and on 5 July 1924 Mrs Henry Ball performed the opening ceremony. Wesley Hall was taken over by the Sunday School which continued to expand until it too needed larger premises. On 29 August 1931, the foundation stone of the new Sunday School was laid by Miss Elizabeth Thompson, the erstwhile organist who had done so much for the early church.

Originally plans were made to include a Methodist day school on the same site as the Church. This plan never materialised because there was no demand for a school. Nevertheless, Bescar Lane Methodist Church continues its ministry today in the northern fringe of the village.

CHAPTER 3

EDUCATION IN SCARISBRICK

From Tudor times until the late Victorian era

HE EDUCATION OF CHILDREN in Scarisbrick is recorded from Tudor times, when Humphrey Cartwright, who had graduated with a Master of Arts degree from Cambridge University, taught in the village. He was ordained in May 1579 at Douai in northern France and returned to England to establish a school for Catholic children in Scarisbrick. Edward Scarisbrick, the lord of the manor at that time, provided accommodation for the Benedictine monk. In return Humphrey Cartwright performed religious duties for the family and educated Edward's children and also those of the Catholic tenantry and of the neighbouring Catholic families. The whole arrangement was clandestine because at that time, it was illegal to practise the Catholic faith. Lessons ended abruptly when Humphrey Cartwright was brought before Gloucester Quarter Sessions and sent to Salford Jail, where he remained for at least ten years.[1]

The secret education of the Catholic children by both Jesuits and secular priests continued intermittently under the protection of the family at the Hall until the passing of the Catholic Relief Act in 1778, which legalised the practice of the Catholic faith. Despite the secrecy surrounding this schooling, it is known that in 1655 Christopher Bradshaigh, son of James Bradshaigh of Haigh near Wigan, came to live at the Hall and taught the Catholic children living in the area. He, like Humphrey Cartwright, was imprisoned for his faith, this time in Liverpool. However, he was able to resume his duties and remained in Scarisbrick until 1674.[2]

The names of scholars who claimed to have been educated at Scarisbrick when they entered seminaries abroad, give us some indication of the years when the secret school was functioning. Charles Cansfield who was born in 1613, was educated by the Jesuits at Scarisbrick, Edward Molyneux attended the school possibly in the 1630s, and Thomas Bannister, John Alcock, Henry Lodge and his brothers were there in the late 1640s and early 1650s.³ Perhaps the best known of the early scholars was John Plessington, who was martyred in 1679, a time of strong anti-Catholic feeling following the plot of Titus Oates. The local priest wrote of him, 'We are proud of the fact that one of the forty martyrs went to school in Scarisbrick'. Robert Wadsworth OSB who trained at Douai in the early 1700s, also went to the school. Many of these scholars wrote their names on their text books, some of which had been published in the sixteenth century, and these remain in the archives at Douai Abbey, now established in England near Wool-hampton. Two scholars, Richard Wilcock and Edward Johnson, wrote their names in books in 1703, so we can presume that the Scarisbrick school was operating successfully in the early years of the eighteenth century.

Later, in the second half of the eighteenth century, the anti-Catholic laws were not applied so stringently and the climate of opinion moved towards tolerating Catholic education. In fact, in 1754 another Catholic boys' school was founded at Ince Blundell under the protection of the Blundell family by a secular priest, Father Boardley from More Hall in Aughton.⁴ Possibly some of the older Catholic boys from Scarisbrick would be among the fifty or sixty boys, who travelled to this school for their education.

The existence of this school was reported to the Bishop of Chester in 1761, but he took no action to close it. A similar attitude was taken by the vicar of Ormskirk in 1778, when he replied to the Visitation questionnaire sent to him by Bishop Porteus of Chester.⁵ There was 'no Popish school kept in the parish . . . that I have ever been informed', but of course the vicar would not be informed officially about the secret Catholic school in the Hall. The vicar did acknowledge that 'Mr Scaris-brick, the Lord of the Manor [kept] a domestic chaplain where the neighbours, his leasehold tenants resort[ed] and assemble[d] for wor-ship'. There is no doubt that the assembling for worship included assembling the children for Catholic education, but the vicar and the bishop again chose to turn a blind eye. In fact, in the following year Bishop Porteus wrote, 'if . . . the schools and mass houses so much complained of, are only frequented by persons of the Roman Catholic persuasion . . . and no doctrines are taught hostile to the government of the country, I do not see how on the principles of toleration and of Christianity, any other opposition can be made to them.'⁶ At last

Catholic education was to be tolerated, even among the highest clerics in the Church of England.

Alongside this clandestine education for the Catholic children of the township, Scarisbrick was also privileged in having one of the earliest Protestant schools in the district. Henry Hill of Scarisbrick expressed his wish to found a school in the village in 1648, trustees were appointed and on 20 April 1648, a piece of ground eighteen yards by fourteen yards in a field called Great Hey at Barclay Hey was conveyed to the trustees, who built a small grammar school on the site. The purpose of this school was to teach English, Latin and Greek grammar to children from the age of seven. The children would be expected to be able to read before they were admitted to the school.[7] Two years later, in 1650, it was described as a 'newly erected chapel'.[8] Evidently the building served as both a school and a chapel during this period, for in the Notitia Cestriensis, a report made to the Bishop of Chester in 1722, it was described as 'a grammar school, built for a Meeting House in Oliver's time – not endowed'.[9]

During these early years, the expenses of the school were met by the local parents, and so it is not surprising that they did not readily agree to pay the £3 6s. 8d. levied on them in 1661 by the Quarter Sessions towards the upkeep of the Grammar School at Ormskirk.[10] When they procrastinated, the constable and churchwarden of Scarisbrick were ordered 'to lay and gather' the money 'and to make undelayed payment thereof', and were warned 'fail not at your peril'.

The financial difficulties of the school were relieved when soon after the Bishop's report of 1722 the Chapel School received an endowment from James Carr,[11] who left 'the sum of one hundred pounds unto the Chapel School in Scarisbrick to and for the advancement of learning and for the glory of God to be lent or set forth upon usury . . . to be a free school. And the interest to go towards paying the poorest chil-dren of Snape and Scarisbrick's learning'. The only other endowment made specifically to the school was another of £100 donated by Mrs Palmer of Middlesex, aunt of Thomas Eccleston of Scarisbrick Hall, on 5 July 1796.[12]

Very few of the names of those who served the school in the early days are known. However, a bond remains dated 1759 whereby the schoolmaster, Thomas Howard, his father Robert, a tailor and William Blundell, all of Scarisbrick make an agreement with the trustees of the

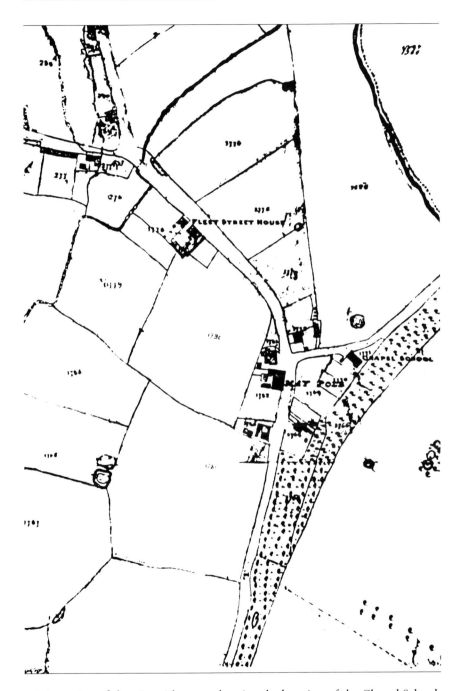

26. A portion of the 1839 tithe map showing the location of the Chapel School. The Maypole was the name of the present Morris Dancers. It is possible that the village maypole once stood near the inn and the old school.

school to repay the sum of forty pounds if Thomas was guilty of any 'neglect or misbehaviour, done, committed or acted contrary to the intentions of the . . . trustees'.[13] The money was Thomas' stipend for the year and the trustees drew up the bond to ensure that it would be repaid if he was dismissed as unsatisfactory, or if he left the school of his own accord. The trustees are listed as Robert Watkinson, Henry Culshaw, James Fisher, James Blundell and James Watkinson.

By 1816 the old school was in a very bad state and the trustees decided to build a new one on the same site. A barn was hired from William Trelfall at the cost of 15s., the children and equipment were moved into it, and lessons were continued in the new venue. Four workmen were paid 2s. 8d. a day to pull down the old school and, in order to raise money for the new school, the old windows were sold for £2 5s. and part of the old floor was sold for 15s. A new brick building was erected and finally, a stone was inscribed with the names of the trustees – an essential part of the project. The cost of the whole operation was £394 9s. 8d.[14] It is significant that Thomas Scarisbrick made a donation of £5 13s. towards the cost of the new building, despite the fact that his family was already subsidising the education of the Catholic children in the township. One of the signatures on the accounts of the new building was that of Thomas Heyes, who was described as a school-teacher in his will dated 1829, and it is very likely that he was the schoolmaster of the Chapel School at the time of the rebuilding.

According to the tithe map of 1839 and also the earliest Ordnance Survey map of the district 1847, this school was located in Bescar Brow Lane in the Chapel School plantation and not, as popular tradition has it, in the tall building opposite the Morris Dancers. A small school house was built alongside the school and the master had the use of the school and school house rent and tax free. In 1818 the master did not want the house, because he already had a home in the village, probably the one tenanted by the Heyes family in 1839 and situated next to a barn (converted into a house in 1994) in Smithy Lane. Consequently the school house was divided into two tenements, and each was let at £4 a year, paid directly to the master. He also received £10, the proceeds of two legacies, on condition that he taught five of the poorest children in the township, free of any charge. At that time thirty children, both boys and girls attended the school. We do not know when the girls were first admitted, but generally, it was not until the movement for

27. The Reverend W. R. Ramsden, first vicar of Scarisbrick.

the establishment of the charity schools in the mid-1700s that girls were taught in schools. By 1851 the Chapel School house was occupied by James Heyes, the school master, his wife Jane, their three children and his sister and brother-in-law, Catherine and James Draper from Halsall. However, by 1861 James Heyes' family had increased to nine children, so he had moved to a larger house in Hurleston Green. John Farrar, the second master, who came from Bury and lost his wife in 1857, moved into the school house and lived there until 1871 with his three children, all born in Scarisbrick, and a housekeeper. A stained-glass window in St Mark's Church commemorates the career of Mr Farrar with the words, 'In loving memory of a beloved schoolmaster 1846–73'.

During the 1840s a school was opened at Primrose Hill, at the junction of the four parishes of Scarisbrick, Ormskirk, Aughton and Halsall. This dame's school was built and sponsored by Mr I. Shaw to cater for the children who lived in these outlying districts. In the 1850s the grandmother of Mrs Elsie Church of Jackson's Common attended the school which was accommodated in the house now known as 'Windy Ridge'. Although there are no specific accounts of the school at this time, the 1851 census records that Jane Kershaw, a school teacher aged 46, lived at Jackson's Common, and as this is very close to the school, it is possible that she was mistress of the Primrose Hill School. By the 1870s there were sixty children on the register and about fifty attended regularly. It was so successful that in 1878, Mr Shaw asked the vicar to appeal to the Education Department to recognise the school under the regulations of the Education Act of 1870. In his letter to the Department,[15] the Reverend Ramsden assured the Authority that the school was well supplied with books, maps etc. and was efficiently taught by a married woman teacher. As Miss Kenyon, she had served as a pupil teacher from 1859, and had acted as an assistant mistress at Halsall school before moving to Primrose Hill. She had not attended a training college and so was not certificated, but the vicar hoped that would not prevent the recognition of the school. However, as there is no record of that being granted, it would appear that it was refused. It is significant that the first attendance register for Pinfold school records that several children had been transferred from Primrose Hill. Perhaps this trend continued and the newer school proved more attractive to pupils. Whatever the reason, by 1910 the school had ceased to function, and now its existence has almost been forgotten.

Forster's Education Act of 1870 required sufficient schools to be established in each area to provide elementary education for all children. When the authorities enquired about the capacity of the existing schools in Scarisbrick, it was found that altogether 123 more places were needed, and it was suggested that 80 more should be provided in the old Chapel School and 50 in a new Infants school. As the existing Roman Catholic School and the Chapel School were both on the western side of Scarisbrick Park, it was decided that the new Infants school, later to become Pinfold school, should be sited at Hurleston, on the eastern side.

The Marchioness offered to provide the necessary accommodation, thus saving the township the expense of establishing a school board – and the attendant taxes which would have been levied to pay for the building and upkeep of the school. She engaged an architect, W. P. Balmer, to enlarge the two floors of the Chapel School to measure 42 ft × 24 ft 6 ins to provide room for the eighty additional places, leaving the heights of the rooms at 9 ft and 8 ft 6 ins. By January 1874, the alterations were complete and the building was in use, but unfortunately, the authorities had misgivings about the heights of the classrooms. The local HMI reported optimistically that the school was well ventilated and provided 'fully 10 square feet per child for the amount of air required', hoping that would satisfy the authority.

The following year the trustees were faced with another serious problem for, after the Board of Education inspection of the Chapel School, the teaching of the headmaster and his wife was criticised so severely that the trustees had no option but to give them notice to leave. They offered Mr Heyes £46 on 7 June on condition that he gave up both school and house within the month. Not surprisingly, he declined and pointed out that, when he was appointed – at least twenty-five years before – it had been agreed that he would be given six months' notice if he was asked to leave. After many arguments and finally with three month's notice Mr and Mrs Heyes left and were replaced by Mr and Mrs Prew in August 1875.[16] All seemed well according to the inspector's report the following year: 'the school premises [have] been put in good order and suitably furnished and, but for their deficient height and the stone floor in the boys' room, the rooms afford ample and fairly efficient accommodation. The master is evidently methodical and efficient and deserves credit for improvement . . .' The trustees, eager to respond to the inspector's suggestion for the sake of the grant he could withhold, asked Thomas Riding of Ormskirk to examine the school and give his opinion as to whether height could be gained by opening the roof to the rafters and whether it would be safe to lower the boys' floor. Riding's findings were reported to the Marchioness and the trustees waited anxiously for her response.

Then disaster struck. Whether there was a different inspector or instructions had been given by a higher authority is unclear, but despite a fairly favourable report in 1877, the inspector reported that from February 1879 the school would cease to be a government school because it did not fulfil government requirements. Its grant would cease, leaving the parish to provide alternative accommodation for the school. Understandably, the Marchioness refused to do anything more to the school, and the trustees were thrown into confusion. Various alternative schemes were proposed, and finally it was agreed that the trustees of the Chapel school should take over the new school to be acquired at Pinfold, and the Marchioness should have the property of the Chapel School and house. She offered to provide a suitable site for the Prot-estants of the township led by Dr Ramsden, who agreed to provide a school to complete the required accommodation.

In the midst of this turmoil in January 1879, Mr and Mrs Prew resigned and their places at the Chapel School were taken by Mr and Mrs Moulding. Later the same year a most damning report was received from the inspector: the 'instruction [is] in such a deplorably bad state . . . the infants are almost as badly taught . . . the sewing is very poor' – a very harsh verdict considering that the Mouldings had only been at the school a couple of months. In fact the inspector was examining the results of the work of their predecessors, which Mr Moulding had also criticised severely when he was appointed. However, by October the new premises were ready, St Mark's School was opened under the headship of Mr Moulding, and a new beginning could be made.

Pinfold School, 1875–1920

Meanwhile, to complete the accommodation required by the Education Act of 1870, the Marchioness bought 'a good building formerly a Wesleyan chapel, not exactly in Horalton Green, but in the neighbourhood and quite well placed in regards to the population',[17] and conveyed it to the trustees of the Chapel School. This school at Pinfold, has been renamed several times, but to avoid confusion I will refer to it as Pinfold school throughout this history.

There had already been a school at Pinfold during the middle years of the nineteenth century. The 1841 census recorded that Elizabeth Hargraves, a schoolmistress aged fifty-five from Anglesey, lived on Southport Road. Her home – and probably her schoolroom – was opposite the present school. By the time of the next census in 1851, she had been joined at her home at Pinfold by William Smith (34), a Calvinistic minister and his wife Mary (38). The Smiths were both school teachers originating from Radnorshire and, as we have seen, William Smith was the minister for a Wesleyan chapel founded at Pinfold in 1849.[18] During their ministry at Scarisbrick, Mr Smith, his wife and Mrs Hargraves, taught children in their new building, the first school at Pinfold. In the 1860s the minister was John Meredith, aged 31, and neither he nor his wife Mary Anne were schoolteachers, although no doubt, they tried to continue the school at Pinfold established by their predecessors. However, the school must have closed shortly afterwards, for none of the children who came to the Marchioness's newly opened school at Pinfold in 1876, are described as having previously attended the Wesleyan school.

When they acquired the building at Pinfold, the trustees altered it as the inspector suggested, a certificated headmistress, Susan Jane Arrowsmith, was appointed and in January 1875 the school opened. Within a few months the attendance had risen to forty-three children. Unfortunately one year later when the school had been established successfully, Mrs Arrowsmith resigned and, although the trustees advertised the vacancy, no-one applied for the post. The trustees decided that their only option was to close the school until a headteacher could be found. Six months later no progress had been made, the school was still closed and the Marquis expressed his deep concern to the trustees. This roused them to action. They re-advertised and eventually appointed Ann Hudson to be headmistress at a salary of £35 per annum. However, difficulties arose when they discovered that Miss Hudson did not have sufficient qualifications to act as headmistress. The authorities agreed to ignore the matter on condition that she sat the examination for the required certificate before the end of the school year and this was done.

Although it had been stipulated that the school should be an infant school, there was some confusion in these early years as to its intended age range. Initially, several older children were admitted, but in December 1877 all the children over nine years of age were asked to leave. Then in March 1879 it was ruled that no boys over seven were to be given places. However, the authority must have had a change of heart, for in 1880 it was decided to admit children over seven. Alterations were made and the school became a mixed school.

The Education Act of 1876 made education compulsory for every child under twelve years of age, despite the fact that the managers were allowed to charge fees. The log book for Pinfold School records that fees were raised in 1877 and all the junior children – those in the second standard and higher were charged threepence a week. This was a considerable sum for a labouring man with a family of six or seven to support and a wage seldom as much as £1 a week. Many opposed the charges, and in 1886 it is recorded 'the children still pay fees against the recommendation' of the inspector. Eventually the following year the pressure of public opinion influenced the managers, and all children below standard V were admitted free of charge. The fee of threepence remained in force for the upper standards until September 1891, when, as a result of the Elementary Education Act, a fee grant was made to schools. This enabled the managers to reduce the charge for the older children in standards V, VI and VII to twopence. Further alterations to the grant system were made in the 1902 Education Act with the result that schooling was then free of charge.

Attendance rose steadily. In January 1877 the average attendance had

28. Inside Pinfold School, 1913. *Back row*: ? Bella Sutton, Nellie Cottam, Nellie Fields, John Church, John Abram, ?, Ernie Prescott, Billie Banks. *Second row*: Nellie Taylor, Mary Ireland, Mary Ellen Longton, Florrie Poole, Janie Fairclough, Nellie Fairclough. *In front*: Lizzie Prescott, ?.

29. Pinfold School, 1917. *Back row*: William Scarisbrick, Nora Prescott, Margaret Church, Alice Prescott, Gladys Prescott, Alice Beardswood. *Third row*: James Banks, May Poole, Belle Glover, Margery Fairclough, Elsie Huyton, Kate Scarisbrick. *Second row*: Alice Darwin, Frances Sutton, Robert Holcroft, Thomas Marshall, Thomas Trudget, Stanley Prescott, Mark Leatherbarrow, George Darwen. *Front row*: Emma Deaken, Jane Sumner, Margaret Kenyon, Jane Farrington, Nellie Abram, Annie Iddon.

been 23, by May 1878 it had reached 54 and by August 1882 that total had more than doubled, causing problems with the accommodation. The headmistress recorded in her log book that she had 'arranged to divide the classroom with a curtain until a new classroom has been built'. Although that might have prevented some of the distractions caused by 110 children being taught in one room, it certainly would not deaden the noise made as they learned to chant their tables and poems or read aloud. Careful timetable planning must have been essential to try to synchronise the noise. This situation continued for over a year and it was not until January 1883 that the trustees decided to invite tenders for the building of a new infants' room. Although the school house at the eastern side of the building was not in use, there was no plan at that time to incorporate it into the school to relieve the overcrowding. In fact, later that year, the cottage and garden were offered to the police for £10 per annum. The trustees must have decided it was essential to keep the house as living accommodation, in case a future headmistress might want to occupy it. There are no accounts of the actual building of the infants room, but it was eventually completed. Attendance continued to be around the hundred mark until the late 1920s when, as the result of national educational policy at that time, the authority decided that the senior children were to be segregated and transferred to Halsall, leaving only 37 children at Pinfold. By the 1940s that number had increased to 60 and there was a slow increase in numbers until the 1960s when, in 1967, the total number on roll reached 71.

Attendance dropped severely when epidemics hit the school. Measles, mumps, whooping cough, chickenpox and scarlet fever took their toll, spreading rapidly through the classes. The only remedy available at that time was to close the school until the fever had run its course. When this happened, the whole school was scrubbed down, disinfected and often lime-washed in an attempt to eradicate the germs. In 1879, when there were about 55 on the roll, the headmistress recorded, '37 present in the morning, 32 in the afternoon, 20 absent having measles'. Ten days later the school was closed and the 'summer holiday [was given] a month earlier due to sickness'. The children who were ill, forfeited their summer holiday for, in the opinion of the managers, there was no point in giving another holiday when most of the children had recovered. A year later, in May 1880, it is recorded 'Diphtheria in the area. Four children from school died of the disease'.

The inevitability of the suffering and death of children in the Victorian era and their elders' complete resignation to the fact, are evident in the log books of this period. The omission of the children's names was probably an unconscious effort to de-personalise the deaths, and so to distance the tragedy. Nevertheless, it was impossible to avoid the real dread that the infection might spread. This dread was increased by ignorance about the fevers and their possible side-effects, and no knowledge of any reliable cure for them. This ever-present fear among the parents surfaced in April 1912 when a scarlet fever epidemic hit the school, and the cases increased rapidly until in May the head teacher reported, '34 absent, 32 have sore throats and 16 children are being kept away through fright'.

Immediately after the First World War the school was closed for five weeks when the nation-wide epidemic of influenza struck both the

30. Pinfold School, 1922. *Back row*: Miss Marchington, Stanley Prescott, John Orritt, Stanley Poole, Herbert Taylor, Michael Church, Edward Huyton, William Gradwell, William Beardwood, Miss Johnson. *Third row*: Glady Prescott, Margery Gradwell, Margaret Scarisbrick, Florence Prescott, Margaret Church, Martha Gerrard, Elsie Huyton, Margery Fairclough, Elizabeth Sutton. *Second row*: Eva Mayor, Eva Prescott, Annie Sherman, Margaret Prescott, Kate Parr, Lily Prescott, Annie Prescott, Elizabeth Fairclough, Babs Olverson. *Front row*: Harry Moorcroft, William Mayor, James Church, Richard Gibbons.

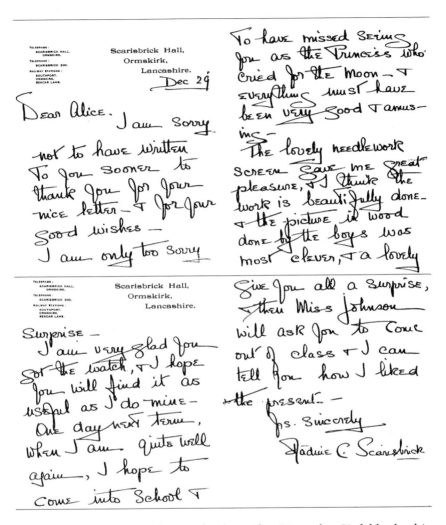

The handwritten letter reads:

Scarisbrick Hall,
Ormskirk,
Lancashire.
Dec 29

Dear Alice. I am sorry not to have written to you sooner to thank you for your nice letter — & for your good wishes — I am only too sorry

Scarisbrick Hall,
Ormskirk,
Lancashire.

Surprise — I am very glad you got the watch, & I hope you will find it as useful as I do mine — One day next term, when I am quite well again, I hope to come into School &

To have missed seeing you as the Princess who cried for the Moon — & everything must have been very good & amusing —

The lovely needlework screen gave me great pleasure, & I think the work is beautifully done — & the picture in wood done by the boys was most clever, & a lovely

give you all a surprise, & then Miss Johnson will ask you to come out of class & I can tell you how I liked the present —

Yrs. sincerely
Nadine C. Scarisbrick

31. A letter written by Lady Scarisbrick to Alice Lingard at Pinfold school in 1938.

children and the staff. Even when the children returned to school, their Christmas concert had to be postponed twice on account of illness. Ringworm was also prevalent in the post-war years, but by this time the children were regularly inspected by Nurse Fry, who sent the infected children home and so, controlled the spread of the infection. Meningitis attacked the school in the 1920s and claimed the lives of two children Martha Gerrard (10) and Belle Glover (13). Then in January 1926 a mixture of infections caused the closure of the school for three weeks when sixty out of a hundred children were absent. It is significant that during the 1920s a great change in attitude occurred. The casualties were named, resignation to infection disappeared and great efforts were made to fight disease. At last there was something actively to be done and suffering was no longer accepted passively as inevitable. Teachers were vaccinated to encourage their pupils to follow suit and vaccination sessions were arranged for the children. Arrangements were made to supply the children with Horlicks malted milk to supplement their diets, which were often unbalanced and inadequate in the days before the spread of health education and income support.

However, despite the frequent epidemics and sicknesses, all was not doom and gloom at Pinfold School. After it had been opened a year, Lady Scarisbrick provided a tea-party for the children and started, what was to become, an annual event in the autumn and a highlight in the life of the school. Despite all their personal difficulties, the family from the Hall maintained a keen supportive interest in the school until the outbreak of the Second World War. Lady Scarisbrick frequently presented prizes at Christmas time and, when school inspectors advocated a broader approach to education – thus releasing teaching from the close confines of the classroom – the grounds of the Hall were opened for nature rambles, visits to the greenhouses and sports days. Royal occasions and national events were also celebrated with festivities in the grounds. For instance, after the coronation of King George and Queen Mary a tea-party was provided, sports were organised with prizes for the winners, and each child was given a medal, a coronation mug and a bag of sweets. Shortly afterwards, in 1912, when the royal couple visited Southport, the children were taken in horse-drawn wagons to watch them pass, and afterwards they were given buns and Ormskirk gingerbread, again provided by the Marchioness. At the end of the First World War peace celebrations were held in the grounds of the Hall.

The children also celebrated more personal events with the Scarisbrick family. When Count Andre, son of the Marchioness, brought his bride home to Scarisbrick Hall, 900 local children were invited to the festivities, as we will see later. The schoolchildren also joined the family on sad occasions as on 11 September 1911, when they attended the funeral of the Marquis. These close links with the family continued until the approach of the Second World War. In 1938 Lady Scarisbrick's illness is recorded in the log book, and the following Christmas, when the younger Lady Scarisbrick had presented prizes at the school, the scholars gave her some needlework done by the girls and sent a knitted cape to the dowager Lady Scarisbrick. That was probably the last occasion when the family had personal contact with the school, before their home became a wartime hospital and they moved away. The almost feudal relationship between the family and its youthful 'tenants' – the children in the school that they had provided – was broken.

The children enjoyed other treats besides those supplied by the Scarisbrick family. When tea-parties or trips were arranged by the Church or by a benevolent association, the school was either closed early or the children were given a holiday, so that they could join in the celebrations. For instance, many of the children attended Sunday School and when the centenary of the movement occurred in 1880, the children were given a holiday. Representatives from the Band of Hope called regularly to speak to the children and the organisation funded several tea-parties for them. The Southport branch of the Oddfellows organised a 'juvenile trip' and again a holiday was given. However, not all holidays from school were for pleasure, seedtime and harvest meant that extra hands were needed in the fields and the children were enlisted to help – until the attendance officer began to enforce the law more stringently from the 1920s onwards.

Wartime

Both the First and the Second World Wars affected the school, and even through the pages of the log book, the difference in attitudes to the two wars is evident. On 7 September 1914 it is recorded that 'the top classes were taken to Gorsuch Lane to see the 250 recruits (several local) from Southport pass on their way to Seaforth Barracks'. To be a soldier was a glorious thing, an ambition to be nurtured, and if local boys volunteered, they were to be cheered on their way. When the wounded heroes were brought to Southport, the school collected produce and sent gifts to them at the Grange and Woodlands VAD hospitals. Concerts were given both to amuse the soldiers and to raise money for medical supplies, socks, mittens and footwarmer covers were knitted, and one Saturday in 1916 sixty of the children were taken on horse wagons to visit the hospital, tour the wards and have tea with the soldiers. Finally, in September 1917, their support for the five hundred wounded soldiers at Woodlands was acknowledged when a bed was named 'The Scarisbrick School bed'.

Despite the jingoism, there were signs that wartime conditions caused hardship. In the cookery centre – opened in the end room of the building 1913 – economical dishes were introduced in 1915 to combat food shortages, and the children were taught to make such things as haricot mutton gruel, potato cakes, fish cakes and meat and potato pies. By 1917 increasing numbers of wartime dishes were on the menu, including tripe and onions and stew with suet balls added to increase the bulk. Great attempts were made towards the end of the war to make the few foods that were readily available more attractive by teaching the children to use recipes for such dishes as sago shape, fish pie and barley broth. They were also taught how to bottle fruit to improve their winter diets. During the latter part of the war the cookery centre was also used to provide meals for many of the children whose parents were finding it difficult to cater for them.

In 1917 when food shortages were making a great impact on the ordinary civilians, it was decided to sacrifice part of the playground for food production. The ground was dug over, and potatoes were planted for use in the school kitchen. It seems strange to us that throughout those grim years, it was the glory which war and serving in the forces brought in their wake, and the privilege of being able to contribute to that glory by collecting and making things or even growing vegetables, that was impressed upon the children. When it was finally over, a Roll of Honour was unveiled and the children sang *The Better Land* and *The Land of Freedom, Land of Glory*. Life gradually returned to normal and by the early 1920 richer, seasonal foods such as mincemeat, Christmas cake and even toffee were on the menu at the cookery centre.

It was different in the Second World War. Then the reality of war came to Scarisbrick and the children themselves were in the front line. They were prepared for gas attacks with regular gas mask drill, for incendiary bombs with regular fire drill. Nets were stuck over the windows to avoid the danger of flying glass and when the alarms were heard, the children were shepherded into the 'refuge room'. Evacuees moved into the school from areas thought to be more at risk, and in May 1941 the school was used as a rest centre for those fleeing from the bombing of Liverpool. Police officers and army captains came to the school and warned the children about unexploded bombs and other dangerous objects to be found in the vicinity. This time war was not glorified, it was feared. Holidays were given when peace was declared, each child was given the King's 'message to the children' and there were celebrations in the village, but as far as the school was concerned, peace was welcomed with relief and thankfulness.

The experiences of the teachers

Since 1876, the teachers have recorded their experiences in the log books, and have given us an insight into their own worries and difficulties. In the early years, the HMIs with their powers of giving or with-holding grants, loom threateningly over the work of the school. Their verdicts on the school's performance were awaited with dread by both the teachers and the managers. When the inspectors threatened to reduce the grant, panic seized the whole school and the headmistress was the one to be blamed. To counter these attacks the head teachers cultivated a defence. During their first weeks as headmistresses they wrote notes in the log book criticising the state of the school – the result of the previous regime. Then if blame came, it would not fall entirely on them. In 1876 Miss Hudson 'found the children rather backward, three only being able to read or write' – out of six and after the school had been closed eleven months; in 1880 Miss Clayton wrote, 'I find this school on the whole very backward in arithmetic . . . very backward in geography'. When he visited the school, the inspector took a wider view of the situation and complained, 'The intelligence of the children has not been sufficiently cultivated'. It seemed as if the teachers could not win. However Miss Clayton and her assistant mistresses did receive hard-won praise many years later, in 1909, when she received – and recorded the fact – a rare letter of appreciation from a parent, J. R. Widdup Esq. for the splendid educational results of his two sons.

In the early 1900s there were many aspects of teaching which would be condemned by modern educationalists. PE was based upon military drill and on 11 February 1910 a Sergeant Major Wright visited Pinfold to examine the children and to give advice to the teachers. Great demands were made on the children's stamina, for instance in 1910, the junior children walked to Ormskirk, were taken around the historical monuments in the church and then walked back. The five-mile journey was repeated in May the same year, when they were taken to Ormskirk to buy plant pots with money they had subscribed, and carried the pots back with them – no such thing as school buses in those days! On the other hand they were expected to sit still and to concentrate on their lessons for long periods of time in cramped desks. As late as 1912 the inspectors found it necessary to advise the teacher to give the infants more freedom, and also a break after every two lessons. These lessons would probably have been an hour long, and the little ones would be confined to their desks throughout that time.

However, modern ideas were gradually introduced with the encouragement of the HMIs who, following the alterations in the grant system in 1891 and 1902, had adopted a more advisory role. Teachers were encouraged to take their lessons outside the classroom, for instance nature rambles were introduced and in 1910 some of the boys went swimming in Southport Baths; in 1911 others visited the Liverpool museum and went aboard the *Saxonia*, a Cunard liner. In 1915 new equipment was introduced to increase the impact of lessons on the older children who learnt to use a microscope. New subjects such as French were introduced to increase the scope of the children's lessons, and even their physical education was modernised as maypole dancing was added to the curriculum. They watched the demolition of the waterworks chimney and were encouraged to explore their rural surroundings. In the early 1920s they were taught using such advanced methods – for that time – as magic lantern lectures and gramophones. Gone were the days when the children were confined to their desks and taught to recite tables, poems, dates and all kinds of sterile information by rote.

St Mark's School

The early log books of St Mark's School describe in detail the difficulties encountered by the various headmasters as they tried to educate the children under their care. Parents, absentees, inspectors, builders and planners, as well as the Temperance Band, the Church Army Mission and at times even the vicar, seemed to conspire to disrupt the life of the school and exasperate the headmaster.

After the school had been open about three months, a parent complained 'because her child was beaten for pushing another child down and beating it when it was down'. The headmaster must have felt the injustice of her intervention, so he recorded the upsetting incident in his log book. A second parent made another unjust complaint in 1898, because the head had sent the attendance officer to her home about absenteeism. This parent responded by saying that she would not send her boy to school on washing day no matter how often she was fined. Unfortunately she did not give her reasons, and we are left to wonder whether she needed his help, or whether the boy had only one outfit for school and so was compelled to be absent until it was washed. Actually, this parent's principal intention seems to have been to harass the teachers, for a week later she 'sent word that no matter what her boy did, she would not have him punished'.

As at Pinfold the inspectors' reports were anticipated with panic. When the inspector's visit was imminent in 1880, the managers under the leadership of the Rev. Ramsden decided that scripture should not be taught until after the exam. In its place the teachers were to concentrate on the subjects in which the children were most backward. School was to begin at 8.45 a.m. and the Rev. Ramsden examined the children a few times before the fateful day. Their dedicated efforts were successful, for the report came through, 'considering the difficulties the Master has had, the school must be considered to have advanced considerably in instruction . . .' This was great praise, and afterwards both the teachers and the children were able to relax into their normal routines. However, the headmaster, Mr Moulding, left soon afterwards and was replaced by Mr Sackfield, who refused to re-organise his work to prepare for the inspector's visit. Consequently he received the report that 'the children have passed a very indifferent exam . . . there is no evidence of good teaching, The infants are backward and under little control', and at the conclusion of his report, the inspector threatened to withdraw the grant. However, once the Board of Education's grants were based on the number of children attending the school,[19] the situation improved. Mr Sackfield, who remained at St Marks for only a year, was followed by dedicated teachers who spent increasingly long periods at St Mark's. In fact in the present century thirty years has been the average length of service of the head teachers, and this stability has led to sustained improvement in the standard of education offered by the school.

However it must be said, that the inspectors did consider the welfare of both the scholars and the teachers when they suggested various structural improvements to the managers, who were similarly pressurised to meet their requirements. This happened in 1895 when water closets were installed and water piped into the school and school house, after the inspector found 'the state of the offices unsatisfactory'. The old gallery (platform) was removed and a raised floor was put in the infant's room in 1899 to accommodate more desks in response to the inspector's suggestion. In 1900 a new gallery and wainscoting was ordered for the classroom, but although the work was planned to be done over the Easter holiday, the contractors did not complete the work in time. All the children except the infants had to be taught in one room, resulting in yet another very harassing time for the teachers as they tried to teach about eighty children in one room – there were 109 children on the roll at that time.

The County Planning Department caused great concern to the head and managers in 1900, when they proposed building a fever hospital only 250 yards away from the school. The headmaster's main anxiety was not the risk of infection, but the fear that the parents' dread of infection would cause them to remove their children from the school. He attended a public enquiry and successfully influenced the final outcome. The fever hospital was built in Moss Lane, North Meols, a good distance away from the school. Illness was a constant worry in St Mark's, as it was at Pinfold School. In 1891 the headmaster himself had to be isolated, because his son had caught diphtheria, and the school was closed for several extra weeks in the summer. The boy recovered, only to die two years later, probably a victim of the measles epidemic which swept the school that year. Similar precautions were taken against the spread of infection as at Pinfold: 'August 18th [1893]. The school floor is again being scrubbed to keep the place as pure as possible'. There is a most depressing series of entries in the log book during the 1890s: 'closed the school early to attend the funeral of a scholar', 'the funeral of our late monitress', and 'my child's funeral'. Again in the early years names are not recorded and then in 1899, a little earlier than at Pinfold, the entries change and the victims are identified: 'Mary Foster who was at school last week was buried yesterday. The infants all brought 1d. each with which a wreath was bought and sent to her mother, and 'Willie Twist, St I, who was at school on Tuesday morning died today after a day's illness. He has been very hoarse for several weeks'.

Epidemics and illnesses interrupted the headmaster's scheme of work, but other cases of absenteeism also disrupted the schedule and retarded the scholars' progress. As at Pinfold, the children were kept at home 'weeding carrots' (1882), 'assisting in the hay' (1889), 'illegally employed (1897), 'beating for the Hall shooting party' (1899) and 'getting potatoes' (1900). Storms also interrupted work, as on 11 December 1891 when the school had to be closed – 'the fires were so smoky that what children did turn up were constantly coughing'.

Outside organisations hiring the school hall, often left a trail of dirt and damage. In 1888 the Temperance Band concealed the fact that they had broken a window, and the headmaster had to make contact with them to get it repaired. After a parochial tea-party in 1897 school arrangements were also 'somewhat upset . . . owing to the platform being left up and a classroom locked up with the remnants' of the party. After the flower show held that same year, the school had to close because it needed 'a thorough washing and cleaning'. Perhaps the worst offender was the Church Army Mission in 1898, when the head-master was forced to complain that 'the displacement and the destruction of the school furniture caused through the nightly mission services, has rendered school work most awkwardly inconvenient'. These were some of the severe disadvantages of being a church school and a suitable meeting place.

However, there was only one headmaster, who according to the log-book openly clashed with the vicar. The Rev. Ramsden took a great interest in the school he had been instrumental in founding, frequently visiting it and, as we have seen, was not averse to taking part in the teaching. However, in 1881 the headmaster Mr Sackfield, who stubborn-ly refused to alter his routine, also objected to the vicar's presence: 'The Reverend Ramsden called again this morning and created much incon-venience and greatly obstructed school work by interfering in the mark-ing, booking and collection of fees'. Then four days later the children did not arrive for school because of something said by the vicar at church on Sunday. This was too much; the headmaster resigned, but the final word in this clash of personalities went to the vicar who wrote in the logbook, 'The school managers have been very much annoyed and dis-satisfied with Mr Jack Sackfield's conduct during the last three months'.

The headmaster was forced to call on the police for help twice during the 1890s. On one occasion the girls' porch was raided and a brown Scotch plaid jacket, a leather satchel, an umbrella and two black shawls were taken – shawls being the usual outdoor wear for girls at that time. Two years later 'a young woman visited the school and took one of the scholar's dinners'. The head caught her and handed her over to the police. Possibly she was the same person, who had found an easy way of relieving her needs in the days before social security.

Holidays and treats were very similar to those at Pinfold with the exception of the tea-parties given by the vicar and his wife and also the week's closure in December 1893 to celebrate Dr Ramsden's twenty-five years at Scarisbrick Church. The teachers showed the same reaction to war in the early days as those at Pinfold The children had a holiday to watch the volunteer review at Southport in 1880, and holidays were also given to commemorate the Relief of Ladysmith and Mafeking in the Boer War. During the Great War eggs were collected for the VAD hospitals in Southport. In fact the collection amounted to as many as 1,566 eggs in 1916. After the war this project was continued in aid of Southport Infirmary. The Second World War brought evacuees and many traumas and difficulties, but the school – and its headmistress –

32. St Mark's school, 16 March 1905. The headmaster was Mr Wilford. His wife taught the lower standards and Edith Margaret Smith taught the infants.

33. St Mark's school in 1917. The first on the second row is Annie Meadows. The teacher in the centre is Miss Wilford, who was a pupil teacher and later went to college. Her father was the headmaster.

34. St Mark's school in 1920. The second on the first row is Annie Meadows. The second on the back row is Thomas Church. The teacher is again Miss Wilford.

emerged ready to continue to face the many, possibly more mundane, disruptions to their work in the late twentieth century.

St Mary's School

Although we recognise that Scarisbrick is a rural community, it is only when we read the logbooks of St Mary's school that we realise how difficult it was in the early years to provide an education for children in this scattered area. The large distances the Catholic children had to travel, usually on foot, affected their attendance. As the teacher complained (2 February 1894), 'I find there are a good number of children in the district who are old enough to come to school, but who have not yet put in an appearance. The parents say it is impossible for them to walk the long distance before they are six'. Later, when she had

35. The infants at St Mark's School in 1979 with their teachers, Mrs Emily Bycroft and Mrs Beryl Evans. *Back row*: Wendy Houghton, Madeline Colvin, Stephen Carr, Kevin Chattaway, Mark Krinks, Gary Rimmer, Jeanette Roberts, Jennifer Howarth, Brian Seddon, James Haslam, Anne Jennings, Annabel Denton, David Fillingham, Leanda Jackson, Jonathan Williams, Alex Jennings, Simon Mangham. *Front row*: Lisa Barton, Stephen Howarth, Lyndsay Bates, Daniel Kershaw, Gail Butterworth, Karl and Stephen Bates, Andrew Marshall.

experienced bad weather in these remote districts, she could appreciate the parents' point of view – 'The attendance at this time of the year is unavoidably poor owing to the severity of the weather and the very long distance the children have to walk, some of them three or even four miles'.

The children's way to school was often along footpaths and unmade roads across the reclaimed mossland surrounding Martin Mere and the other mosses in the area. Consequently, even a rainstorm could have disastrous results, as on 11 October 1872, when 'in some parts of the village the roads [were] impassable . . .' or on 10 August 1898 when there were 'only three children present, no school during the morning. This [was] the result of a tremendous downpour of rain which . . . rendered the roads impassable for the little ones'. Snow caused even greater problems, as in the winter of 1909–1910 when the school had to be closed early for the Christmas holidays because 'the roads were blocked with snow and no traffic of any kind could be carried on. The children were unable to travel to school'. In fact until the 1920s weather conditions frequently affected attendance so badly that the school was forced to close.

Nevertheless, it was surprising what an effort the children made to get to school. In March 1909 several infants arrived after a snow storm, only to be sent home 'many of them . . . sick with cold'. The head teacher was amazed how persistent his scholars were in November 1923, and recorded 'attendance 92% for the week in spite of heavy rain every morning. Several children walked four miles in blinding hail and sleet on Friday morning'.

Consequently the children often arrived very wet and bedraggled and measures had to be taken to dry them, as the teacher noted on one occasion (4 September 1875) 'only nineteen children made their appearance, their clothes were taken off and dried and they were dismissed as soon as the weather permitted'. Drying clothes could be a problem as in March 1878, when school was dismissed because 'it not being safe to keep the children in their wet clothes, the fires not having burnt up sufficiently to dry them', or even as late as 8 September 1932, when 'fires had to be specially lit in order to dry the children's stockings etc.' In 1878 a disaster followed this drying-out process as the teacher recorded, 'On Monday, a child putting her boots on the stove to dry, let them remain too long and they were destroyed'. That day there must have been an even more horrible stench than the usual dank smell of drying clothes in the schoolroom.

Warming the large schoolrooms was a problem in the early days, so when a new room was built in 1893 for the infants, one of the chief benefits was the new 'heating apparatus' – an early central heating system. The teacher noted, 'when the smell of the paint vanishes, the room will be extremely comfortable and warm'. Later the new heating had far-reaching effects for it became 'a great inducement for parents to send' their little ones to school. Nevertheless even the central heating could be a victim of the weather, as in 1912 when the pipes froze in the extreme cold and the ink froze in the children's inkwells.

The shorter hours of daylight in the wintertime affected work in the school. Each November the girls' needlework lessons had to be altered 'because they [could] not see after three o'clock'. When December came the children were sent home at 3.15 p.m. instead of 4 p.m. 'as it was too dark to work after that time' (11 December 1895). These conditions persisted until 1937 when electricity was installed in the school.

Before the passing of the Education Act in 1870 it was usual for children in rural areas to work seasonally in the fields alongside their parents, and this custom was hard to break. In June 1872 the teacher observed that 'many of the boys kept at home to work in the fields and will probably not return again till after the harvest'. Consequently, the teacher had only the winter months to get those children up to standard and yet when the inspector came to examine them he would expect them to have made the same progress as those who attended regularly. For the next fifty years these absences continued to be a problem. The children were employed in every kind of agricultural work. They reaped corn, they gathered fruit, they made hay, they sowed grain in addition to setting and picking potatoes. If they were either too young or too weak for any of those jobs, they would be kept at home to carry lunches and teas into the fields for the workers.

In the end the managers were forced to admit that the demand for the children's labour was so great at certain times that the best policy was to close the school for a short holiday to cater for the need. Consequently, in 1908 and each following year the school was closed for a week in the autumn for potato picking, and the Easter holidays were lengthened by several days so that the children could help to set potatoes. During the First World War, when labour was very short,

36. In the playground at St Mary's. *c.* 1915. *Back row*: Nellie Martland, Annie Taylor, Annie Banks (Heaton), Mary Woodcock (Charnock), Dorothy Charnock. *Front row*: Annie Charnock (Ackers), Peggy Taylor (Cheetham), Annie Waring (married names in brackets).

the autumn break for potato picking was increased to three weeks, and towards the end of that war (April 1918), most of the children over twelve and indeed some under that age, were kept at home for about six weeks in the spring to help with the sowing and the planting. In the 1920s the authorities tightened the restrictions governing child labour, and attendance officers were more vigilant.

A popular rural pursuit enjoyed by the monied classes interfered with the children's schooling in the early years of this century. When the Casteja family organised the annual shoot in November, they enlisted many of the children to act as beaters. Some of the older residents in Scarisbrick still remember this break from the usual routine – as we shall see in the last chapter.

Despite all these disadvantages of being a rural school, there were several distinct advantages and the teachers at St Mary's exploited these to the full. Nature study walks and rambles were organised as early as 1902, so that the children had practical experience of many aspects of botany and biology. In fact these rambles were a very necessary supplement to classroom work, for in the classroom the teacher often had as many as seventy children to teach at one time. Individual tuition was impossible in that situation, whereas in the fields each child could find specimens to examine on his own under the overall supervision of the teacher.

This stimulated the scholars' interest in nature study, and led them to submit wild flower entries to Southport Flower Show. The first time this happened was in 1909, when the school was closed at midday to enable the children to go to the show. Later in the year, the Mayoress of Southport came to school and distributed the certificates and medals won by the children. As the teacher recorded, 'Several gold, silver and bronze medals were bestowed on the children and I must say I am very pleased with them'. The scholars' interest continued at least until 1936 and probably much longer, but in these later years the school was usually on holiday at the time of the Show, so the events were not recorded in the log books.

In 1931 a school garden was established with the help of Mr Steer, the County Horticultural Advisor. An area of 1,200 square yards was measured off a nearby field, and the boys dug it in readiness for planting potatoes, with the intention of supplying the school kitchen. The Education Authority provided a toolshed, a wheelbarrow and a set of tools, the potatoes were set and after great care they yielded a very good crop. That autumn the garden was divided up into plots and each boy in the gardening class was made responsible for cultivating his own plot. After a year Mr Swarbrick, a school manager and a professional gardener, judged the boys' work and awarded prizes for the best results. Miss Richmond, headmistress 1930–60, was very enthusiastic about the gardening project, and supervised the planting of fruit trees and roses. She also arranged to have a trellis erected for climbing roses. The boys were taught how to prune fruit trees and roses by Mr Steer, and later the same year (1933) they went to a local nursery to learn how to bud roses. For many years the gardening classes continued to be a great success and gained well-deserved praise from visitors and also from the inspectors, who were especially impressed by the course on grafting and by the detailed records kept by the boys.

Miss Richmond was not content with teaching only gardening techniques to her country children. She decided to extend the rural aspect of her teaching and to make a contribution to the war effort by including poultry keeping on the curriculum. In March 1940, a hen cabin was erected alongside the girls' playing field and the following month she recorded, 'Great excitement prevails today. Fifty day-old chicks have arrived and have been put in the brooder house'. A poultry club was formed and the boys were divided into groups to tend the birds. Accounts were to be kept and once expenses had been met, dividends were to be paid out of the profits. Their optimism was replaced by horror as one by one the fledgelings died, until only twenty-nine survived. Miss Richmond decided to investigate the reason for their deaths, and sent the bodies away for a report. Evidently a rare disease of the gizzard had caused their deaths, and when she informed the suppliers, they replaced the dead chicks immediately. The following November the children's labour was rewarded when the pullets began to lay. However, another set-back came when poultry food was rationed, but the group were able to supplement the allowance with scraps and peel from the school kitchen. The poultry continued to produce eggs throughout the wartime years of food shortages.

Bee-keeping was also introduced as a wartime measure in 1941. A grant of £5 was obtained, the bees and equipment were bought and in the following December Miss Richmond was able to report that 32lb of honey had been produced in the first year. The school joined the Beekeepers Association and so, when the bees swarmed they could get expert help if it was needed. By 1944 there were three beehives including one demonstration model in the school garden among the fruit trees. The honey provided a very welcome sweetener to eke out the sugar rations and helped to relieve the monotonous diet of wartime.

Wartime at St Mary's

The records of St Mary's School provide a most detailed account of the coming of the Second World War and of all the consequent disruption of the day-to-day life of the school. Neither the head teachers of St Mark's nor of Pinfold School recorded their experiences so vividly, but they must have endured similar conditions.

The account begins with the warnings and plans of September 1938 – 'Should a state of emergency be declared (war being imminent) all schools must be closed until further notice'. Then a note of panic crept in, 'ARP drill in order to evacuate the children as soon as possible when necessary, was carried out three times today', – three times was rather excessive. Relief was uppermost after Neville Chamberlain's return from his meeting with Hitler, 'The crisis has passed, war has been averted, so ARP drill etc. is no longer necessary'.

The next year there was no escape from the inevitable as Miss Richmond recorded on 28 August 1939, 'there are rumours of war'. Then three days later the BBC commenced the role it was to play for the next five years, the direct means of communication between the government and the people. 'Several broadcasts have been made asking all schools to stand by at 2 p.m.' The broadcast message was that all schools must close until further notice as a state of emergency had been declared. The headmistress decided to use the opportunity to prepare for the possible arrival of evacuees, and set her staff the task of clearing cupboards to make room for any equipment they might bring with them.

Another period of indecision by the authorities followed. 'Official notice received and contradicted during the past fortnight, that evacuated children would be sent to the village and would attend this school'. The billeting officer decided to ignore the wavering and made arrangements for the evacuees reception 'if and when' they came. Eventually on 14 September the evacuees arrived: 135 children from Holy Trinity Roman Catholic School (juniors) and St Francis' Roman Catholic School (seniors) in Garston, Liverpool. Miss Richmond was involved in billeting the children and opened her own home to the headteacher and first assistant of Holy Trinity School. The local authority issued instructions that St Mary's was to open each morning from 8.30 a.m. until 12.30 a.m. and the evacuated schools were to have the use of the premises between 1 p.m. and 5 p.m. In those circumstances Miss Richmond decided to reorganise her timetables, reducing the time allotted to games, handwork and art. It was also decided that only one day's holiday – a day of religious observation – would be taken in October on account of the long emergency holiday taken in September. ARP drill and gas mask drill were taken regularly.

Both boys and girls spent much of their free time knitting articles for servicemen, and on 21 December when Lady Scarisbrick and several of the managers came to the school for the annual prize-giving, the children presented the knitted goods to Lady Scarisbrick. She was 'obviously surprised and delighted with the presentation' and no doubt would distribute them later among the wounded soldiers in the hospital at the Hall. As Christmas-time approached the parents collected money for a children's party. On Christmas Day both the evacuees and the local children were given a dinner party and in the afternoon the local children gave a concert for the evacuees 'and all had an enjoyable time'.

Dissatisfaction with the shift system of teaching surfaced in January, and Miss Richmond told the County Organiser that if more equipment could be provided to cater for the increase in the number of midday meals, there was no reason why the schools could not be amalgamated. However, little was done because a severe blizzard, 'the worst in living memory', caused more immediate problems. Snowdrifts cut off large areas of the parish and the school had to be closed for a week. An entry in the log book on this occasion illustrates Miss Richmond's typical concern for her pupils. Before sending home the few children who had made the journey through the snow, she made sure that they were given an hour of 'folk dancing to warm them' on 29 January 1940.

Nothing was done about the proposed amalgamation and so, on 13 April, the Head teacher visited the Education Office demanding that some action be taken, as parents were complaining about their children receiving only part-time education. The following week the required equipment was bought, and on 22 April the schools were amalgamated into five classes instead of the customary four, Miss Nugent, one of the evacuated teachers taking the extra senior class. Three weeks later, when the new classes were settled into a routine, she was recalled to teach in the Liverpool school and was replaced by an infant teacher. Reorganisation was necessary yet again.

Suddenly the war came very close, as bombs dropped on the village during the summer holidays. As soon as the children returned to school, an air raid practice was held. No shelters had been built at this stage and so the children were lined up in the corridor where it was thought they would be safe. The Education Authority provided anti-splinter net and the teachers spent their break carefully fixing it onto the windows. Six weeks later we read 'most of the anti-splinter net fixed to the passage windows . . . is now hanging limp and useless because of the damp'. The Liverpool teacher who had to be on duty over the Christmas holidays, took her Christmas break after the school opened again, leaving the school with another staffing problem requiring more re-organisation. New private evacuees were admitted to the school, while those from Garston gradually returned home. Progress was impossible in such frustrating conditions.

Then the May blitz hit the area. Bescar station was hit and several other places nearby suffered. Orders were sent out to black out the school in readiness for it to be used for refugees. The teachers and a team of local workmen blacked out the windows and skylights, but no refugees arrived. A fortnight later it was decided to take down the black-out. At seven o'clock the same day the refugees arrived. Workmen were engaged to blackout the school more permanently and it became an official rest centre. The day school was closed by order of the medical officer of health. A band of volunteers cared for the refugees giving them food night and morning, and each night the refugees – sometimes as many as thirty-eight, sometimes only about twelve – arrived from the bombed areas. After a week at St Mary's they were transferred to Pinfold School. The following morning according to the log book, 'the school was sprayed with disinfectant by the health authorities, after which it was thoroughly cleaned and made ready for the children'. That crisis was over.

It was still necessary to be prepared for the worst, so on 14 January 1942 a police sergeant from Ormskirk and a senior air raid warden came to the school and examined the children's gas masks, replacing damaged ones or any that the children had out-grown, and supervising gas mask drill. Finally a full ARP drill was taken. During these early years of the war all children carried their masks to school each day, while their parents vied with each other to create the most attractive and serviceable covers for the mask's mundane cardboard containers.

The school played an important part in the various National Savings Campaigns. The headmistress chronicled her experiences of Warship Week in mid-February 1942. On the first day she explained that, as the school would be one of the centres where money would be deposited, she would be unable to give her undivided attention to the work of the school, but would be 'much occupied with financial matters' and this certainly proved to be true. The following day she supervised the deposit of £80 which was brought by the children to be put into the school bank. Then two days later she had to go to Ormskirk to bank over £1,000 paid into the savings scheme. On the Friday she sent one of the staff on the same errand with over £2,000, and the bank was so busy that it was four hours before she returned. Later that afternoon Dr Calland, a district councillor, and several of the school managers came into the school to present one of the senior boys with a savings certificate for making up a winning slogan in a savings competition. The visits to the bank continued the following week, and altogether £8,459 18s. 10d. was raised for the National Savings. The following year (1943) the Wings for Victory campaign was even more successful increasing the previous total by £2,000. Salute the Soldier week in 1944 and Thanksgiving week in 1945 each resulted in the school raising over £10,000, a truly wonderful effort – thanks to the commitment of Miss Richmond.

Practical help towards the war effort was given each year by the children, who worked in the fields during the potato harvest. In 1942 the need for help in the fields was so pressing that it was decided to allow the children to work during school time and to regularise the situation. Cards were issued to children over twelve allowing them to work in the afternoons during a maximum of twenty school days, and the cards had to be signed by the employer to guard against truancy. A total of sixteen boys and girls from St Mary's decided to increase their pocket money by taking advantage of this scheme, which was continued until the end of the war.

By the end of 1943 most of the Liverpool evacuees had returned home and in December the official register was closed, only a few private evacuees and about four of the official Liverpool ones remaining. However the problem was not over for in August 1944, flying bomb attacks were launched against London and the South East. Several families from that area were evacuated to Scarisbrick, bringing thirteen children to St Mary's School. After a few months the danger subsided and seven of the children returned home, the rest staying until the following June.

May 1945 brought VE day and the school was closed for a national holiday. No great celebrations were organised by the school, but there were celebrations for the village at the Hall. Finally only four of the evacuees now remained – 'the children having no mothers to make homes for them to go to'. However to end Miss Richmond's account of St Mary's wartime experiences on a less sombre note, a typical incident occurred in November 1945. The Public Assistance van called to collect the blackout frames which had been up at the school windows during all the latter years of the war. When the headmistress suggested that they could be used when films were shown to the children, she was told to send ten shillings to the Committee to pay for them – the school's paltry reward for a tremendous war effort.

However, Miss Richmond did receive some recognition for all her work for the War Savings movement when she was invited to attend the royal garden party at Buckingham Palace on 5 June 1946. The managers decided that all the school could share in the celebration by having a day's holiday, when their headmistress – and indirectly all the people of Scarisbrick – were honoured for their great efforts to support the country during wartime.

37. A class at St Mary's with Father Philip Robinson in 1977. It was taken on their first communion day, when they returned to school for breakfast. They are wearing their first communion medals. *Back row*: Michael Church, Carl Hilton, Chris Griffin, Andrew Naylor, Mark Ashcroft, Michael Lenaghan, Michael Molyneux. *Front row*: Matthew Shutt, Terry Griffin, Sharon Dobson, Elizabeth Horner, Sammy Horner, Sharon Blundell, Mark Charnock.

CHAPTER 4

MEMORIES OF SCARISBRICK

HE FINAL CHAPTER OF THIS HISTORY has been collected from today's people of Scarisbrick. It has been compiled from the memories and souvenirs of the older generation and the recollections of those who have lived through the more recent events of the twentieth century.

The most surprising fact that has emerged from the many, many hours I have spent talking to those who remembered old Scarisbrick, was that without exception, they have stressed how happy they were, what fun they had during their childhood and what satisfaction they got from their work. Many historians viewing this period from today's perspective would stress the dreadful conditions endured by the under-privileged masses as they were exploited by their capitalist masters. The paternalistic attitude of the family at the Hall would be condemned as a means of forcing their tenants to comply with their wishes, and of increasing their own wealth by taking advantage of this compliance. Certainly this is one interpretation of the facts, but perhaps a less damning view of the way of life of our forefathers is valid. It is impossible to deny that those who have experienced the harsh condi-tions and have lived through that very difficult period, view their lives in retrospect as full of contentment and happiness. Perhaps this is only a trick of the memory, or perhaps modern inventions, especially radio and television have not brought the anticipated contentment in their wake. By enlarging the horizons of ordinary folk and increasing their awareness of contemporary problems and events, they have also in-creased people's worries and expectations and have destroyed their ability to enjoy life to the full.

The earliest local evidence of contemporary attitudes to national events in the late nineteenth century, comes in a booklet produced to celebrate the Diamond Jubilee of Queen Victoria. It was dedicated to the Count and Countess de Casteja 'as a mark of appreciation of the kind and liberal interest taken by them in the children's treat and gala

38. Lady Anne
Scarisbrick, born
1788, died 1872.

held in Scarisbrick Hall'. In these words the committee members under
Richard Sefton of Drummersdale Mission expressed their genuine feelings of gratitude to the family in the Hall. Neither was there a hint of
dissatisfaction or criticism of their Victorian government in the description of the Jubilee day as a 'golden link between our nation's wonderful
past and its, may we not hope, still more wonderful future'. Some
would condemn this as a blinkered view of the Victorian Age, and
maybe it was, but this was contemporary opinion expressed by the
worthy committee.

At the local level the hope was that 'the men and women and children
of different shades of opinion in religion and politics, who on that day
were as one in their rejoicings, may long, long be united in the bonds
of true amity and friendship'. Echoes of a less united past emerge here,

as times are recollected when Protestant informed on Catholic, when Parliamentarian fought Roundhead in the battles around Lathom House, and later, when Jacobites in the township supported rebellion against the Hanoverian monarchy, but these traditional differences were forgotten in the the Jubilee celebrations. The family at the Hall was also included in the wish for the continuation of the status quo – 'may the noble family . . . long enjoy the confidence and esteem which they deserve'. This was an expression of the tenantry's true feelings of loyalty and gratitude towards their landlord at that time.

39. The Marquis de Casteja, born 22 February 1805, died 11 August 1898.

The committee chose to celebrate the occasion with a pageant, copying on a tiny scale the great Jubilee procession of foreign princes and dignitaries to St Paul's Cathedral in London, and described the event in their booklet. Nearly six hundred children assembled at Bescar Lane school. The girls, dressed in white, walked two by two and were followed by the boys and then by decorated 'lurries' carrying the very youngest children. The horses had ribbons plaited in their manes and tails, and even the drivers' whips were bedecked with ribbons. Banners were carried, and each child had a Diamond Jubilee medal pinned on his chest. On arriving at the Hall each child was given milk in a mug donated by the Countess. There was a 'punchinello' – Punch and Judy – show and a display of decorated wagons, some of which were quite ingenious. One tiny donkey pulled a coster cart with a small cask displaying a notice 'Non-intoxicating;a cure for red noses'. In front on the donkey hung a bunch of carrots suspended on a long pole. The proximity of the carrots controlled the speed of the cart. Cyclists were included in the fancy dress parade; one represented a man o'war and another a Parisienne lady in bloomers. Nathan Sefton was dressed as a village policeman demanding 'Home rule for Scarisbrick' – perhaps the only hint of a discordant note in the celebration and, for us, a reminder of the Irish troubles in the nineteenth century.

Meanwhile, the children had 'a capital' tea paid for by public subscription, followed by sports. There was every kind of race not only for the children – including the girls in their, once snow-white, dresses – but also for the adults. The indomitable Richard Sephton won the one mile flat race, and when darkness fell there was a firework display. Finally everyone left for home exhausted with happy memories of Jubilee Day, 21 July 1897.

The next festive occasion celebrated by the parish, was the homecoming of Count Andre de Casteja, eldest son of the Count, and his new wife, Pauline daughter of the Marquis d'Espeuilles, after their marriage and honeymoon on the continent. On 22 August 1898 the newly-weds travelled from London by rail to Liverpool and then changed on to the Cheshire Lines to travel as far as Altcar. There they changed again for the journey to Halsall, and this time the carriage was pulled by an engine of the Lancashire and Yorkshire railway, specially decorated for the occasion. The station was festooned with banners and a large archway with the words 'Welcome Home' on it had been erected over the entrance. On the platform were the official guests, while many of the local inhabitants lined the roadway and bridge, intent on catching a glimpse of the bride and welcoming her to her new home. Children carrying banners from Halsall and Haskayne schools lined the road from the station and waited to welcome the couple. As the train drew in sounding its whistle, cheering erupted from the crowd, and when the couple alighted, speeches of welcome were made by several of the local dignitaries. Count Andre caused even more cheering by his response that as a Lancashire man, he was pleased to return home to live among his own people. The whole scene was captured on a film 'manipulated' by a member of the staff of Archer & Son of Liverpool.[1]

All along the route to the Hall were decorations of every kind, and at the Ormskirk Lodge entrance to the Park, children from Pinfold School lined the roadway. The carriage stopped at the bridge over the ornamental lake, where Richard Sephton, then Chairman of the Parish Council, welcomed the couple on behalf of the people of Scarisbrick. Then something happened which seems more akin to television fiction than to life in nineteenth-century Scarisbrick. The horses pulling the carriage were unhitched, ropes were attached to the carriage and fifty stalwart tenants pulled it to the front entrance of the Hall. There more local dignitaries including representatives of Ormskirk Urban District Council, awaited the couple to present their good wishes. At last when all the speeches had been said, the family and their close friends retired to the Hall, while the tenantry – 350 people – and the various deputations were entertained for lunch in large marquees on the lawn. In the evening the celebrations spread to Aughton, where William Rothwell fired a salute and lit a huge bonfire on Clieves Hills in honour of the bride and bridegroom.

The following day children from the three townships on the estate – Scarisbrick, Halsall and Haskayne – were invited to a celebration in the Park. It began with a procession from the Round Lodge to the Hall, where the family were waiting to receive them together with most of the tenantry from the estate. As the procession reached the Hall, a band struck up with the tune of *Home Sweet Home*, and everyone joined in the singing of a song written specifically for the occasion by Reverend Blake of St Mark's Church. Then the procession, led by morris dancers from Ainsdale, re-formed. The younger children rode in decorated wagons lent by various farmers, while cyclists in fancy dress followed in the rear, all wearing the medals given to them in commemoration of the marriage. The procession dispersed when it reached a field near

40 & 41. The medal struck to commemorate the wedding of the Count and Countess Andre de Casteja in 1898.

42. The children of the Casteja family riding in the grounds of the Hall.

the Round Lodge, and the children were given tea in the open air, while the adults had light meals in some of the marquees. Various entertainments had been provided to please all ages; hobby-horses delighted the little ones and pierrots performed in a dell in the Park for the older folk. Later, sports with generous prizes for the winners were organised and in the evening the band played for dancing until dusk. The whole celebration was long remembered by those who took part, and souvenirs of the occasion are still treasured by their families.

When the Scarisbrick family lived at the Hall, they allowed the grounds to be used for sports days and agricultural shows, and once a year they invited the tenantry to an open day to wander around the gardens and see the orangery. This was an occasion when the villagers – always dressed in their best clothes – could spend the day imagining what it would be like to be rich and privileged. All too soon it was time to return to reality, go back to their farms and cottages and resume their normal daily life.

Most of their homes were very simple with few concessions to comfort. The lower rooms had stone floors, which many of the house-proud women scrubbed daily with Bath stone or Monkey Brand to lighten the colour of the flags. In some homes, a white border about twelve

No. 101

Mr. *Charles Scarisbrick Esq* *the* Landowner,
Mr. *James Hooton* Occupier. } **D**ʳ

To CHARLES SCARISBRICK, ESQUIRE.

	£.	s.	d.
To One Year's Tithe Rent Charge payable 1st July, 1854, and 1st January, 1855, on *13* A. .. *1* R. .. *37* P. of Lands in the Township of Scarisbrick.	0	.12	.8½
Arrear brought forward			

£ *0 . 12 . 8½*

1855, January,   Received the above Sum for
CHARLES SCARISBRICK, Esquire.

43. A tithe rent receipt for 1855.

inches wide was scrubbed around the fireplace with yet another kind of rubbing stone. Sometimes this border was extended all around the room, but as anyone who stepped on it left footprints, few busy farmhouse kitchens received this treatment. In the working rooms, silver sand was sprinkled over the whole floor to fill up the cracks between the flags, absorb any spills or wetness and so make the floor easier to clean. The silver sand was brought from a quarry on Scarth Hill in Ormskirk by Tommy Winrow, who was known locally as 'Sha'. He sold it around the village in bucketfuls from a flat cart. The farmers' wives were so proud of their spotless floors that stories about them have been passed down to younger generations. One told to me concerned the stonemasons who built St Elizabeth's Church. They lodged at Culshaw's farm off Bescar Lane, and often used to compliment the farmer's wife on her spotless floors, saying that they could have eaten their dinners off the stone flags.

Stone floors were very cold and so rag mats were made by the cottagers to put under their feet, when they sat in front of the fire. Of course some of the floors were left bare, and according to tradition in one cottage where three spinster sisters lived, the floor had been worn into three hollows – one in front of each of the sister's chairs. The irons on the soles of their clogs had rubbed the stone away. The furniture in these rooms was simple; a large table – again well scrubbed – white wooden stools, upright chairs with cushions, cupboards on both sides

THIS NOTE TO BE PRESENTED ON PAYMENT.

CHEQUES TO BE PAYABLE TO THE MARQUIS DE CASTEJA, AND CROSSED
MANCHESTER & LIVERPOOL DISTRICT BANK, SOUTHPORT."

Scarisbrick Hall.

Nov _____ 1905

M*rs* Alice Culshaw

To The Marquis de Casteja D*r*

To ½ _____ years Rack Rent
due Aug 2*nd* 1905 for Cottage
in Scarisbrick _____ | 4 | 5 | 0

Water Rate
Pole Rate
at Rate

Arrears

Received by M P Wolfenden
on Nov 22*d* 1905 £ | 4 | 5 | 0

Payment is requested at the Rent Audit which
will be held at Scarisbrick Hall Estate Office
on Nov 27*h* 1905 _____ between nine and one o'clock
previous to which any error in this account should
be corrected at The Estate Office Scarisbrick Hall.

RENTS OF £5 AND OVER SHOULD BE PAID IN NOTES OR BY A CHEQUE.

44. A receipt for the rent for a cottage in Scarisbrick, 1905.

of the fireplace and the inevitable iron firegrate and oven, where the family's meals were cooked.

The toilets – or rather the closets – were down the garden. They were dry and many were made with two holes – one intended for the child. Ashes from the fire were tipped down as required, and when the closet needed emptying, the contents were shovelled into a barrow and put on the midden with all the other household refuse. When the midden – an open pit – was full, the contents were taken and spread on the land. Actually the midden was little different from today's compost heap and an early example of recycling which is so popular nowadays. Even in the larger farmhouses conditions were similar, and it is interesting to note that dry closets were in use in some of the local schools until the 1950s and bucket closets until the 1960s.

Several of today's senior citizens told me about their schooldays in Scarisbrick before the Great War. Their days used to start with a good breakfast of either porridge made from oatmeal – not porridge oats – or pobs made from bread soaked in milk. Cereals were unknown in their homes. Jam and bread followed, or bacon and egg, or bacon and some other cooked food. While they were eating, the men's 'baggin' was prepared. Slices of bacon and an egg, or food similar to what the children had eaten, was put onto an enamel dish, thick slices of bread were laid on top and the whole meal was tied in a red spotted handkerchief. The children then took this meal, together with a can of tea, to the workers who had been in the fields since day-break. The labourers usually returned to the farm for their lunch, a cooked meal of potatoes, bacon, ham or some other meat. Then at about three o'clock yet another meal of an egg and bread and butter was taken out to them. The boiled egg was often put into the can of tea to keep it warm. Sometimes the meal included a piece of fatty cake (pastry) with a slice of pork in it. Certainly the farm labourers of that day could not complain that they were hungry.

Sometimes these 'baggin' deliveries to the fields caused problems for the children, especially when the menfolk were unloading manure boats, because that involved the children in a long walk to the wharf. The mothers used to explain the difficulty to the teachers at school, and then the children would be allowed to arrive at school later than usual. If scholars lived near a main route, the farmers would often give the smaller ones a lift to school on their wagons. The older boys learned

LICENCE
FOR

GN 6396

ONE CARRIAGE (drawn by Horses or Mules or by a Motor Car) at 15s. 0d.

* *George Cooper*

of *Snape Green* in the

Civil Parish or Township of *Scarisbrick* within the

Administrative County † _____ of *Lanc.*

is hereby authorized to keep ONE CARRIAGE with *less than four wheels* to be drawn by a Horse or Mule or Horses or Mules, or, if of a weight unladen not exceeding ONE TON or exceeding FIVE TONS, to be drawn by a Motor Car, from the date hereof until the *31st day of December* next following; the sum of FIFTEEN SHILLINGS having been paid for this Licence.

Granted at *Ormskirk*

this *8* day of *Jan* 191

by *O Parry*

*Note.—Name to be inserted in full.
†If the residence is within a County Borough strike out "Administrative" and insert "Borough" after "County".
S. D. 1913.

45. George Cooper's carriage licence for 1914.

46. A group of flower sellers outside the Morris Dancers. On their return to Southport from Ormskirk market the wagonette drivers used to stop at the inn to water their horses. The flower sellers would cluster around the wagonettes shouting 'A penny a bunch'. On the left are Pollie Porter from Bullens Lane and Lizzie Banks from Saddlers Row.

to jump on to the back of a wagon and get a ride when the driver was not looking. Southport Road was a favourite place for a similar prank on the way home from school. Wagonettes used to take visitors to Southport either from Ormskirk or from the canal passenger boats. The boys used to jump on to the back step, hoping that the driver was unaware of his extra passengers. Then there would be a flick of the whip across the back of the wagonette, and the boys were liable to be knocked off their insecure perches. Cadging rides could be a dangerous hobby.

If there was no 'baggins' to deliver, the children were able to spend more time on the journey to school. Some of them used to go along Southport Road to Snig Pot Brook, opposite Bullens Lane, to watch the huge steam wagons fill up with water from the brook. Two wagons used this water regularly: one belonging to Outrams the bakers carried flour; the other was a freelance wagon. Other children spent their extra time trundling iron hoops along the byeroads. Many of these hoops were made for the children by Jimmy Jump, who had a smithy in Bescar Lane near the Methodist Church, and lived in the tall house opposite the Morris Dancers.

The local children played all kinds of simple games using whatever was at hand. For instance Piggy was played with sticks. A pointed stick was put in the ground and the group would try to hit it from a distance with other sticks. For a similar game, Duck Stones, rounded pebbles were used. A large stone with a smaller stone on top of it was put in the centre of a ring of children. The game was to try to displace the top stone by throwing small stones at it. Another game using pebbles was jacks and bobber. This involved throwing up the bobber and picking up a jack until all four jacks were in your hand, and then reversing the process. If a jack fell on the ground, your opponent took over and tried his skill. Yet another game involved picking up buttons by licking your finger and pressing it on to a button to lift it. The one who lifted the most buttons off the ground, was the winner. Some games involved flicking cigarette cards against a wall or contests arranged as to who could flick them the furthest. Similar games were played with marbles. Children invented games using the most unpromising materials. Schoolgirls had a widely accepted routine for the games they played each season. Skipping was played in the winter, whip and top in the spring, hop scotch in the summer and hoops in the autumn.

I suppose the deciding factor was keeping warm in the playground, but it is strange that all the girls, even those in other distant Lancashire villages, accepted a similar routine.

Most of the children stayed at school for their lunch, because their mothers were at work either in the fields, in the Hall or in one of the other large, local houses. In fact, several of the mothers walked to Ormskirk to do housework for the wealthier people in that town. The children who went to the Pinfold School, used to take cans with milk, sugar and tea, and a meat and potato pie with them. These were put into special cupboards in the school. When it was nearly dinner time, the cans were taken to the lady next door to the school, who filled them with boiling water – 'scalded' them – for one penny. If the child wanted to warm a pie, the lady put it into her oven and charged twopence for the service. There was a similar custom at the village school at Haskayne, so it probably was the usual practice in many of the country schools. In the 1930s, Mr Wright – 'Cakey' – exploited this custom by calling at St Mark's school two or three times a week with hot meat and potato pies and cakes in his basket. He sold the pies to the scholars for twopence and the maid-of-honour cakes for a penny each. However, at St Mary's school midday meals were cooked on the premises for the children from as early as 1929, and cost only threepence a day. That ensured that most of those children had at least one good meal a day.

When school was over, some of the younger children played out with their friends, but most of the scholars had tasks to do. During the winter days, one of my informants was expected to light the kitchen fire as soon as he got home ready for his mother's return from work in the fields. While it was burning up, he had to prepare a large pan of potatoes and put them on the fire to boil for the family's dinner. Another used to hurry out to the fields to lead the chain horse, the extra horse needed if the ground was heavy for ploughing, or if the three-horse binder was being used. This freed a labourer to do heavier work in the fields. According to the seasons, other children stooked the corn, helped with the hay ricks and did countless other jobs suitable for young hands.

Then, usually as darkness fell, the family gathered for their main meal together. The fare was very simple in most of the cottages. Potatoes were the staple food and were served in many different ways: boiled, baked, roast, mashed, as chips or scallops, fried after mashing or, of course, as that all-time favourite, grated cake. This was made by grating potatoes into a bowl, salting them and letting them stand. The water that gathered was poured off, a handful of flour was added and then the mixture was baked in the oven. When it was cooked, it was cut into slices. Sometimes these were eaten straight from the oven, or fried and dipped in sugar to eat as a sweet. Another simple treat was bread soaked in milk and fried. The hot slices were then either dipped in sugar or eaten with a little salt as a savoury. Marrow slices soaked in salt and fried after the water had been absorbed, were a popular meal. Often the poorer families could not afford to give their children meat each day, and so they had chips served with onion sauce. However, many of the families had bacon, often from a pig they had reared themselves. When the pig had been slaughtered, the housewives used to cure the meat – bacon for two weeks and ham for three. Some of the women used a time-honoured method to keep blow flies off the meat, and covered the hams with whitewash to preserve them. When the time came to eat the meat, the white wash was cracked off leaving no trace of preservative. Sunday was the day for a large roast served with some of the many vegetables grown in the gardens. The remnants of cold meat were served for several days afterwards, either for dinner or for the workers baggins.

There were the usual treats at Eastertime and Christmas. Shrove Tuesday was so important that in 1880 St Mary's school even had half a day's holiday in preparation for 'pancake making'. The children were expected to eat vast quantities of pancakes and were threatened 'we'll put you on t'midden if you don't finish that lot'. At Christmas the families had either a goose, a duck or a joint of pork, all either reared at home or by a neighbour or relative. Turkey for Christmas dinner was unknown in Scarisbrick in the early 1900s.

On Good Friday the children went pace egging. That involved going around the neighbours, many of them relatives, begging for eggs to boil and colour for Easter Sunday. In the early nineteenth century most people kept hens, and when the children called, they were usually given one or two to take home in their basket. If the demands became too much, some of the grumpier farmers would say, 'Eh lad, t'cock hasn't laid today'. Sometimes the children would be led by one boy known as 'Toss Pot', who was dressed in a suit covered with pieces of rag or ribbons, and a top hat. Although no-one can remember it happening in Scarisbrick, it is recorded that in Aughton on Good Fridays at the turn of the century, a play used to be acted by the visiting children carrying wooden swords. During the action, one of their number pretended to be wounded and a doctor was summoned.[2] This custom originated in medieval times in the miracle plays, which were performed on carts in market places throughout the country. Several of these plays are still presented in York and Chester, but in this area they were abandoned by adults. Nevertheless, they remained part of the folk memory and were perpetuated by the children's plays. On Good Friday in the early nineteenth century, Ormskirk children used to act the story of St George and the Dragon in their neighbours' houses, when they begged for eggs. By the twentieth century, this play had been abandoned and St George had become Toss Pot. A generation ago, Toss Pot disappeared, and now even the begging for eggs has been abandoned.

Holidays as we know them were only taken by the rich. Nevertheless, local children enjoyed their days out to Southport as much as many enjoy their trips to Spain today. The mothers would pack up sandwiches, and the whole family would catch a train to Southport from Bescar Lane station. Once in Southport they would head for the beach. The little ones would make sand castles, have rides on the donkeys, or paddle in the sea, while the older ones would play football or cricket on the sands. As a special treat they would visit the fairground and ride on the roundabouts or try their luck at one of the booths. Trips to Southport were also organised by the various Sunday Schools, but on these occasions the children were usually taken in wagonettes. Some of the teenagers spent their free time in Southport, but others used to enjoy sports locally. The older boys used to collect at the home of Evan Heaton, Ball's Farm, where there was a football pitch in the pasture. Evan took a great interest in sport and provided the boys with all kinds of equipment. A croquet set was housed in a hut alongside the lawn and boxing gloves were kept in the loft over the barn. In the wintertime when the canal froze, the children and many of the adults had a great time skating and sliding on the canal.

The girls used to go to dancing classes in the evening at Pinfold school. They had a quick tea at one of the nearby houses, and then rushed back to school, where one of the teachers stayed behind to teach dancing. When they were older, both boys and girls used to cycle to Birkdale,

47. Mr and Mrs Sharrock outside Hurleston Hall around the turn of the century.

where Miss Callan taught dancing. She used a wind-up gramophone for music, and charged only threepence a lesson. The adult villagers also enjoyed dancing and the local schools often held dances to raise money for good causes. The Sharrock family of Hurleston Hall were particularly fortunate in having a large hall, where they could hold dances. Their home was an early black and white Tudor building constructed around a central hall, which probably dated from an earlier date than the rest of the building. The father of the family had married Anne Grizedale, who had been headmistress of Pinfold school, and they had six sons, two of whom died in infancy. One of the boys, Evan, learned to play the accordian and so was in great demand to play for dancing. Whenever there was an excuse, the Sharrock family would open their doors, and invite all their neighbours to join in the fun. The Heaton family of four girls from the bakery opposite to the Red Lion Inn, were always welcome to partner the Sharrock boys. Unfortunately Evan was killed in the First World War and the family lost their enthusiasm for dancing.

Before school-leaving age was raised to fourteen in 1900, most children left school at twelve. Those who were destined to become farm workers, often followed the age-old custom of leaving home and going to live in the farm where they were to be employed. Mr Banks of Wood Lane, Bescar told me about his father's experiences of living at his workplace. He slept in a garret with the other farm labourers and was woken before daybreak. After a mug of tea and a piece of bread – or toast if he was lucky – he went into the fields, not to return until dusk.

48. Evan Heaton's van outside the alms houses in Hall Road in the 1900s.

The farmer's wife, who had a reputation for carefulness – or meanness – had a meal ready for them. She never put the loaf of bread on the table, instead she used to ask incredulously, 'Durst a want another?' before she got up from the table and cut the required piece of bread. This happened each time more bread was required until the boys were too embarrassed to ask for more. She knew what would have happened if the hungry teenagers had been allowed to help themselves.

Mr Banks senior was very interested in working with horses, and when he was older, he became a teamsman earning between twelve and fifteen shillings a week. Later when he could be trusted to look after the horses at the weekend, he was paid an extra shilling a week. When he married, he moved into the farm cottage now lying derelict on the road to Burscough, and became an expert at controlling horses. Whenever ploughing competitions were organised at the various agricultural shows nearby, he competed and won many cups and prizes.

An important part of the farmers' work was fertilising the fields or 'muck spreading', and the Scarisbrick farmers were particularly fortunate in having an immense source of manure available in Liverpool, where it could be loaded on to barges and brought by the canal directly to Scarisbrick. After the streets were cleaned, the manure from hundreds of draught horses that worked in the city, was taken to the Corporation yards, where it was stored with night soil from the many urban middens.

1815.

WINDLE

THE PROPERTY OF

T. SCARISBRICK, ESQ.

To Cover this Season,

At Scarisbrick, near Ormskirk,

LANCASHIRE;

Blood Mares at Five Guineas each, and Ten Shillings and Sixpence the Groom.

Other Mares at Two Guineas each, and Five Shillings the Groom.

N. B. Mr. Scarisbrick's own Tenant's Mares, at half price, and 5s. the Groom.

WINDLE was got by Beningbrough, his dam, Mary Ann, by Sir Peter; grandam by Marsk; great grandam by Match'em; great great grandam by Belgrade.—*Vide General Stud Book.*

He will attend at the following places during the Season:—On Monday morning, at nine o'clock, at the Old Roan; from thence to Mr. Gregson's, Hackin's Hey, Liverpool, and stop there all day on Tuesday:—on Wednesday morning, at nine o'clock, at Derby Chapel; from thence to Prescot; and stop all night at Mr. Cowling's, St. Helen's:—on Thursday morning, at nine o'clock, at Rainford; from thence to Wm. Rimmer's, the George and Dragon Ormskirk; and the remainder of the week at Scarisbrick Hall.

Good Grass for Mares at Scarisbrick Hall, and proper care will be taken of them at Seven Shillings and Sixpence per week.

☞ Money to be paid at or before Midsummer, or before the Mares are taken away.

R. COCKER, PRINTER, ORMSKIRK.

---

49. An advertisement for a stud at Scarisbrick Hall, 1815.

This mixed manure was known to the farmers as 'black muck' and, as it often contained such things as broken bottles and crockery, it was sold at a cheaper price than the 'better muck' which came directly from stables in the city. Later, this manure was sold to farmers as a fertiliser, and was spread on the fields, where today the broken pottery and glass from the 'black muck' often comes to the surface. Each farmer negotiated his own terms with the authority at their office in Water Street, and in return the farmers often supplied hay for the Corporation's working horses. One of elderly residents of Scarisbrick has happy memories of being taken to this Liverpool office by her father and, after he had ordered the manure he needed, being taken to see the floating landing stage at the pierhead. Other sources of manure were the many private stables and cowsheds in the city. Again the barges would take hay for the city animals and return loaded with as much as sixty tons of manure. When the barges arrived in Scarisbrick, all the farm workers were extremely busy with their wheelbarrows 'gettin a bowt muck aht'. It was very important to turn the boat around quickly, so that the return load of hay or produce could be dispatched to the city to be sold. While all this work was going on, the horses rested in stables reserved for the manure horses at Heaton's Bridge. Sometimes manure came from similar sources in Manchester, and then it would be delivered by canal via Wigan, or by the railway to Bescar Lane station.

Manure was particularly important for the potato crop. It was taken to the fields and dumped in piles along the drills made earlier by the ploughman. Then unskilled labourers 'knocked muck', spreading it evenly along the drills to be covered over with soil later by the plough team. Many of these labourers were Irishmen who came over each spring to help with work on the farm, and returned home in the autumn. Often they lived in 'paddy shants' – cottages or outhouses – near the farm or, if they worked near Ormskirk, in lodgings in the town centre. When the manure was covered, the women moved into the field and planted the 'sprits'. These pieces of potato with an eye (a bud) on each, had been prepared by the women and older children in the early spring. As they planted, the women usually worked with a labourer who dug a hole, the woman slipped a sprit into the hole and the man removed his spade and covered the plant. This was the routine for early potatoes; the main crop sprits were usually put directly on top of the manure. When manure was bought in wintertime, it was spread evenly over the whole field in readiness for the many other vegetable crops such as cabbage and sprouts grown in Scarisbrick. In fact one of the local farmers, Mr Huyton, was known as the Sprout King because he grew so many fields of them.

Much of the produce went by canal to Wigan market, where there was a great demand for fresh vegetables. The barges took the produce – and the farmer's handcart – to the wharf at Wigan. The farmers followed very early the following morning by train from Bescar Lane station. They went immediately to the wharf, loaded their produce onto their hand cart and trundled it into the market. Other farmers sent their produce to Liverpool. Their teamsmen walked all the way, leading the horses until they reached the city, where stables catered for the market horses. The teamsmen spent the night in the stable, while the farmers if they had followed later, stayed either in a simple boarding house or shared the stable. Some farmers left Scarisbrick as early as four o'clock in the morning for it was essential that they were in the market very early to claim a stand in a good position. When they had sold their produce, they returned to Scarisbrick with several other farmers travelling in convoy, the one carrying the money bags driving the centre wagon for safety.

Later, marketing methods changed and large produce merchants started to buy produce directly from the field. Martland's of Burscough Bridge bought potatoes and grain in bulk and stored them in their warehouse at Bescar Lane station. Thomas Ball, who took his threshing machine around to different farms, often bought the grain he had threshed, and took it back to his store. Moore's collected produce in wagons from the farms and took it directly to their retail outlets.

Some farmers dealt in animals as a sideline. Mr Eddie Scarisbrick's father bought horses from remote areas in Wales or in the Pennines, and arranged for them to be transported to Ormskirk by train. The horses were trained on his farm and then he sold them on to other farmers or bargemen.

Many of the cottagers made a living selling vegetables, flowers and herbs grown in their own gardens. Several of the gardens covered an acre of ground and so they were able to produce a viable amount of vegetables. The cottagers put their produce into skips, large wicker baskets, for sale in the nearby markets. Some loaded their skips on to flat carts and wheeled them into Ormskirk for the Thursday or Saturday markets. Others preferred to send them by canal to Wigan. They would trundle their handcarts containing the skips down to the depot at Heaton's Bridge where both skips and handcart would be loaded onto the barge. Then the same procedure would be followed as that of the larger producers. When motor wagons were introduced, the routine was altered. The wagons would call round at the cottages to collect the skips, the handcart and often the grower as well. In the evening cottagers and handcarts would return on the lorry after an enjoyable – and profitable – day at the market. Ormskirk was the favourite venue for those who had eggs for sale. They were carried in wicker baskets with wicker lids to keep the eggs from harm. The wicker baskets were made locally from the twigs of the willow trees which grew alongside the dykes in the mosses. When the skips were past their best, they were used to collect any refuse which could not be spread on the fields. This was taken to a pit opposite Olverson's farm in Smithy Lane and tipped.

Once the wintertime arrived, all this activity came to an end. Farm labourers were laid off until the spring, and the farmer and his sons would spend their time repairing walls and hedges, and ensuring that the ditches were clear in time for the winter storms. Flooding was an ever-present threat to the farmers on the reclaimed mosses, even in the summer months. Many a crop was lost and a family's income decimated by flooding until as recently as the 1950s.

The shoot organised by the Casteja family broke the monotony of winter. In November a number of guests were invited to stay at the Hall for several days. As we have read, the older boys of the village were enlisted to beat in company with farm labourers from the farms involved in the shoot. The boys welcomed both the opportunity of a day off school, and the pay – often as much as five shillings a day. That was a considerable amount in those days when one farmer – who shall be nameless – paid his son only that amount for a week's work when he was about to be married. There were other advantages for the villagers from the shoot. A large hot-pot was made in the Hall kitchen and was carried to the farm where the shoot was taking place. The farmer's wife entertained the party in her home, and afterwards the family was allowed to eat up what was left of the hot-pot. I am told that one small girl thought it was extremely good, especially the large lumps of pheasant at the bottom of the pot. When the shoot was over, the beaters were given another meal – this time of bread and cheese – before they left for home.

Although by far the greater majority of Scarisbrick villagers worked on the land, many were employed providing for the needs of agriculture. There were four smithies; one on Southport Rd opposite the Red Lion, one in Smithy Lane, one at Drummersdale and the other at Bescar where Jimmy Jump made the boys' hoops in his spare time. Their work was principally shoeing horses, but they also repaired iron ploughs and any of the other machinery or implements used about the farms. The shoemaker on Smithy Lane accepted any repair work that involved leather work.

Nellie Iddon's grandfather, George Kenyon, worked in the smithy at the corner of Smithy Lane. The horses were shoed in the porch under the two statues. During the nineteenth century it was the custom to place clay pipes in the mouths of the statues and if they fell out or were broken, the smith carefully replaced them. The field behind the smithy was walled with sandstone and people used to take the sandstone and grind it down to use for cleaning their stone floors. At intervals along

50. The Scarisbrick shooting party *c.* 1895 with the Marquis de Casteja, wearing a light coloured suit. The gamekeepers, in their uniform of beige velveteen breeches, are holding poles which they used when vaulting the ditches. The head keeper, William Connington, wore a top hat and the underkeepers wore bowlers. The policeman immediately behind the Marquis is P. C. Clayton.

51. 'The Hare and Hounds' in 1839 and later the old smithy, now a garage.

the stone walls were gateways, and Nellie was told that the ground had once been used as a race-course. On the 1847 Ordnance Survey map the smithy is named 'The Hare and Hounds' and on the tithe map of 1839 the tenant was an earlier George Kenyon. The land behind was called the paddock suggesting that the land had indeed been used for horse racing, probably in the eighteenth century when the sport was very popular and the race-course at Ormskirk attracted many of the gentry. The inn would cater for the racegoers and probably there would be a smithy attached to cater for the horses' needs.

There were also three wheelwrights in the village: one near Heaton's Castle farm, one beside the Morris Dancers and one at Pinfold, which has given its name to the modern housing development of Wheelwright's Wharf. The wheelwright's house at Pinfold was built in 1801 and was the home of the Glover family. It was a small house, and when the wheelwright's family had increased to four boys and a girl, he told the Count that he would have to move to another district because he needed a larger house. The Count valued Mr Glover's work so much that he gave orders to extend the house saying, 'We don't want to lose such a good wheelwright'. It was this helpful attitude of the Count towards his tenants that earned him their respect and bound the community together. Of course in this instance the Count would increase the rent on the property, but that was valid. Incidently Mr Tom Glover, a later wheelwright who also lived in that house, was a member of the first parish council in 1895.

The waterworks on Southport Rd employed several men. In the early 1800s the water had been pumped from the sandstone beds by a wind pump, but later in the century that was replaced by a steam engine installed by the Southport Waterworks Company founded in 1853 to serve a large area including North Meols and Birkdale. The engine was housed in a long low building with a large chimney, and alongside was the reservoir. The site was surrounded with a brick wall and the engineer's cottage stood at the gate. By the 1920s the site was disused and many can remember watching the demolition of the old water-works' chimney when they were children.

The railway, too, was a source of employment for many – maintaining the lines, manning the signalboxes, organising the warehousing, operating the weighing machine as well as working on the trains. Mr Taylor who lived in Drummersdale Lane, was a signalman. He had a large garden and in his spare time, he used to grow onions and sage for a local butcher who specialised in making pork sausages. His wife, a seamstress, found work in Southport. Some skilled craftsmen also had to move outside the rural area and found work in Ormskirk. Mr Banks was apprenticed to a plasterer in the town, and was taught the traditional method of using cow hair in plaster in order to fix it firmly on to the laths. The last smooth coat of plaster was then applied, resulting in the perfect finish required in town houses at that time.

Scarisbrick produced stone and bricks for urban development in both Southport and Ormskirk. In fact an agreement was made between

52. The wheelwright's house opposite the Red Lion.

Thomas Eccleston[3] and John Balshaw, Joseph Law and two other workmen that they would do all the stone masons' work on six dwelling houses in Ormskirk in 1789 and would supply flagging from Scarisbrick delph, dress it and lay it for seven pence a yard. The prestigious hotel, the Royal Clifton Hotel at Southport, was built of Scarisbrick stone, and it is very likely that Smithy house and the many other stone houses in Scarisbrick dating form the early years of the nineteenth century, were also built of stone from the delph at Pinfold. Certainly several stone masons and quarry labourers are recorded in the local censuses.

One of the brick crofts was situated near the present site of New Hall Hospital, and the other was at the opposite end of the parish, near Pippin St Both these works employed many labourers during the early years of this century. A large quantity of clay was extracted from the land on the two sites, in fact the difference in height – about two metres – between the land on the west side of Hares Lane and that on the eastern side is ascribed to the extraction of clay from the land on the western side. The clay which lies in bands across the area, has been used since the seventeenth century for marling fields. By this method clay was spread over sandy soils to make them heavier and to increase the amount of water held by the soil. Many of the water-filled pits in

53. The waterwork's chimney falling during the destruction of the former works in the 1920s. Mill House Cottage is in the background.

the area were caused by the extraction of clay either for marling or for brick-making.

Although the police headquarters were in Ormskirk, the local police lived in the area. Originally Scarisbrick had been policed from the Hall, and in the graveyard of St Mark's Church there is a gravestone erected by the Marquis to commemorate the Constable of Scarisbrick, William Ion, who died in 1879. Another constable who was stationed at the Hall, was John Bowerbank, who lived in Star Cottage on the estate and served for twenty-five years before retiring after suffering three severe strokes. In 1883 the trustees of Pinfold School let the teacher's house adjoining the school to the Ormskirk police to serve as the local police station, and policing moved away from the Hall. Later the station was moved into the house immediately opposite the Morris Dancers, formerly a doctor's residence that had been converted from a farmhouse.

Many people were employed directly by the Scarisbrick family to work at the Hall. Women were employed as cooks, laundrymaids, housemaids and dairy maids, but there was also plenty of employment for men as grooms, gardeners, butlers, gamekeepers and all the labourers required on such a large estate. Gas was made privately to light the Hall, so men were required to operate the plant. In fact there was a

54. The gravestone of the policeman of Scarisbrick Hall.

55. A group of policemen patrolling an early 'car park' at Scarisbrick Hall.

surprising number of skilled men employed in this truly rural area in the early years of the century.

This was to change with the coming of the Great War, when men from all walks of life enlisted in the Forces. Women and children tried to fill the gaps in the workforce, as St Mary's log book recorded (2 July 1915), 'a great number of children have left this war time for work', and later (14 April 1916), 'a great number of the senior children [are] working in the fields'. As we have seen, the children's holidays were extended to cater for the demands for their labour. One of the many Scarisbrick women who took over the responsibility of keeping essential services operating, was Miss Isabel Bowerbank, who ran the Post Office on Southport Rd, near Carr Cross.

Soldiers were stationed at the Hall and trained in the district. When they were marching in the lanes around Snape, they used to stop outside Dobson's Farm where they were sure to be offered a glass of milk. In the fields around Jackson's Common, the soldiers were trained to dig trenches, and again, those who were children at that time, remember being sent by their mothers with tea and sandwiches for the men.

The cavalry and the veterinary unit stationed in the grounds of the Hall, brought unexpected advantages for the farmers. Free manure was available for any farmer who would collect it, and similar arrangements

56. Southport Rd, Scarisbrick. The cottage in the foreground has become a restaurant in recent times. The row of cottages visible behind the tall police house was called Saddler's Row.

applied to the re-mount depot at Lathom Hall. One Scarisbrick farmer, Jack Houghton of White House Farm at Barrison Green, used to get up at four o'clock and take his labourer to Lathom to collect free manure before beginning his normal day's work. One member of the Huyton family was stationed at Lathom Hall with the Royal Artillery. After several years service elsewhere he got this posting described by his friends as 'the back o'beyond'. Huyton did not complain. He applied for a sleeping-out pass and lived at home for the rest of the war. Not many were so lucky.

Wounded soldiers were brought to Ormskirk and treated in the Cottage Hospital. At that time Elsie, the youngest member of the Huyton family, also had to spend some time at the hospital after an operation on her lung as a result of pleurisy. There she was befriended by several of the wounded soldiers, who used to wheel her around the grounds in a wheel-chair. Although she was only six, the soldiers corresponded with her afterwards, and one of them sent her seashells from the Dardenelles. It is poignant to think of that soldier remembering a small Scarisbrick girl in the midst of such danger.

The soldiers used Clyffe's Farm near St Mary's School as a canteen, and when it was home time, the children would cluster around the soldiers begging for cigarette cards. If they were given some, they would swop any duplicate cards with their friends until they had a complete set or, as we read earlier, would make them the basis for many of their playground games.

One local senior citizen remembers the day armistice was declared on 11 November 1918. The children were away from school because their war-time three-week potato picking holiday had been extended by a month, and he was picking potatoes in a field near Gregson's Bridge. Suddenly the horn at Ainscough's flour mill in Burscough started blowing and the bells from the churches in Ormskirk rang out across the fields. Peace had been declared. Great celebrations were held in most homes, but sadly some of the villagers were in the grip of the 'flu epidemic which raged at that time. In fact, the epidemic caused so many deaths that in the Hartley home in Scarisbrick, there were three coffins in the house at one time. When the time came for the scholars to return, only five were well enough to attend school. Fortunately my informant avoided the epidemic, and has happier memories of that time. His earnings rocketed to a record £13 10s. during that potato season. The boys were classified by their efficiency and paid accordingly. As he was a grade A picker and with the advantage of the extended picking season, he had become a millionaire – or nearly!

57. An old steam threshing machine at Cliffe's Farm.

Peace brought advantages to many of those who served in the war. When Mr Huyton returned, he was offered the lease of a field in order to start in business as a small-holder. The family had a horse and cart and so marketing was no problem. Their landlords, the Casteja family, had other difficulties. In 1920, when all the tenant farmers gathered in the Hall for rent day, the Marquis broke the news that he had lost all his money. The farms would have to be sold. The tenant farmers had the option of either buying their own holdings or moving out, leaving the farm to be sold to a syndicate. Unfortunately for the small farmers the price of land had escalated after the war and what had been worth £4 an acre was priced at £8 in the 1920s. John Charnock's family could not afford to buy the farm that had been in their family for generations, so they had no alternative but to move out. Elizabeth Halsall, widowed mother-in-law of James one of the sons, lived alone in part of the tall house opposite the Morris Dancers, and so James and his family decided to move in with her. Mrs Halsall already had a small shop in the eastern part of the house and James opened a post

58. The store next to Jump's house opposite the Morris Dancers.

office in the same premises. The business prospered and after a while, he bought an old shed from the ex-munitions works at Aintree, and moved the shop and post office into it, giving the family more living space in the house. Later his wife converted the other end of the shed into a tea-room and Mr Charnock installed a billiard table. Each evening, the tea-room became a club room where the young people used to gather, play billiards and drink cordials until it was bed time. Unlike today they had no problem with burglaries and never needed to lock the door when they went to bed at night. When this complex eventually changed hands, it was bought by Bob Latham, who delivered groceries around the village in the years before the Second World War. A clinic was opened in part of the tea-room during the 1930s.

The Casteja estate was bought in 1923 by Sir Talbot Scarisbrick, a distant relative of the Marquis, and it seemed as if the Hall would be preserved as a family home. Shoots were organised as before the war and Mr Boulter was employed as gamekeeper. He often slept in the woods hoping to catch poachers by stretching wires between trees, which detonated empty cartridges when they were touched. Mr Boulter lived in the gamekeeper's tied cottage, which had altered very little since the nineteenth century. When Sir Talbot died in 1933, the Hall was taken over by his son, Sir Everard, and Lady Scarisbrick, both of whom continued to take an interest in the affairs of the local community as the Marquis and Count had done before the war. One senior citizen remembers that as a boy, he was invited by Sir Everard into one of the rooms in the Hall where there was a complete lay-out of Hornby trains. His feelings of wonder have lasted until today.

Earlier Moore's, the produce merchants, had bought several of the farms and the smithy at Drummersdale End from the Marquis and had appointed bailiffs to operate their Scarisbrick estate. These bailiffs were very officious, instructing all who worked on their estate to use only the smithy at Drummersdale, whenever their horses needed shoeing or if they needed any other smith's work. Whether it was these attitudes, or whether it was the post-war conditions that were responsible for the Moores' difficulties in finding labour in the 1920s, is difficult to tell, but the result was that they also decided to sell up the farms, concentrate on their produce business and develop retail outlets. Moore's Markets in Southport and Blackpool were born.

Another great change took place in Scarisbrick in 1927, when New

59. The family of James and Josephine Charnock taken in front of Jump's House opposite the Morris Dancers, *c.* 1920. The family are (*left to right*) John, Mary, Dorothy, Leo, and Frank in front.

Hall Hospital for infectious diseases was built. The old hospital in Moss Lane, a corrugated iron building, needed replacing and a new complex of buildings was erected on the land belonging to New Hall Farm. The original farmhouse became the matron's house, and separate buildings were built to provide isolation blocks for such diseases as scarlet fever, diphtheria, tuberculosis and erysipelas. Each ward had a verandah, and was divided into sections with male patients at one end and females at the other with a kitchen between the two. If the weather was fine, the patients were wheeled out onto the verandahs. At that time it was thought that plenty of fresh air could cure tuberculosis, and so those patients spent most of their time outside on the verandahs of the wards or later, of the chalets that were built to extend the accommodation. Waterproof covers were put on the beds when the weather was damp and in wintertime, when the nurses were attending to those patients, they used to wear boots and put topcoats under their capes to keep warm. In the early years the hospital cared for about eighty patients, but later as the virulent fevers subsided and the need for strict isolation passed, more patients could be treated and the capacity of the hospital increased to about a hundred and thirty patients. Most of these came from the area served by Southport Health Board which funded the

60. Lady Scarisbrick opening the Scarisbrick Charity Show in aid of the Welcome Home Fund in 1945. Her husband Sir Everard Scarisbrick is seated behind her and George Ainscough, chairman of the committee, is on the right of the picture. Dr O'Reagan, seated at the front, lived in the Mansion House in Ormskirk and was chairman for the day. The roof of the Milk House – later the mausoleum for Sir Talbot Scarisbrick – can be seen.

hospital, and so it often happened that when Scarisbrick children caught infectious diseases, they were taken to a hospital in Aughton, despite the fact that they already had an excellent hospital on their doorstep.

About this time, the first Scout troupe was founded by Harold Sumner. The vicar allowed the group to use the room over his barn and arranged for electricity to be installed for lighting or whatever other use they had for it. A meter was installed, so that the Scouts could pay for the current they used. However, the vicar insisted that the same shillings were inserted over and over again. Lockers were built all around the room to hold the troupe's equipment and many happy hours were spent in that upper room.

In 1934, several of the older youths of the village, including Eric Charnock and Joe Wright, decided that they needed a clubroom where they could play darts, dominoes or cards during the dark winter evenings. They were full of enthusiasm and distributed leaflets appealing for help for their project. They also approached the Scarisbrick family for support, as many of their predecessors had done throughout the ages. Sir Everard agreed to buy a piece of land in Bullens Lane for them from Ted Tinsley, the market gardener, and to let it to them for the rent of one shilling a year, on condition that no intoxicating liquor was sold on the premises. Although they had collected some money, they had insufficient to buy even the most basic building. Then one of them had a brilliant idea. They could sell the top soil off their newly-acquired plot. They approached Aspinall's of Southport who agreed to pay 1s. 9d. a ton for 200 tons of soil, which they would dig and cart away themselves. From this sale the group acquired sufficient funds to buy a wooden second-hand church hall from St John's Rd in Birkdale. Their last problem was the foundations. The remaining funds would not stretch to paying a builder. Eric Charnock persuaded his employer, Mr Fyles to help. He agreed to build the foundations and wait for payment until the club was established. At last the clubroom could be erected. At first

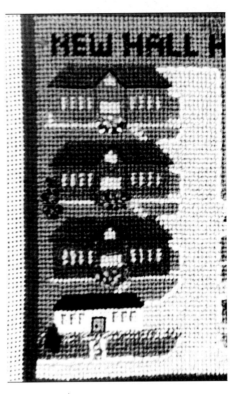

61. New Hall Hospital as portrayed on the tapestry celebrating the centenary of the parish. This part was worked by Betty Armfield.

it was known as the institute and for many years it provided accommodation for all kinds of leisure activities including dances – the only occasions when ladies were allowed into this male stronghold until the days of sex equality in the 1980s.

Then came the war and the old order of things in Scarisbrick disappeared for ever. This war was not to be fought like the Great War, in far distant places. This time one of the most important war zones was to be the home front. The issue of gas masks to everyone including

62. A group of Scarisbrick Scouts in the 1930s. *Standing left to right*: Harold Sumner, Jim Banks, Bill Church, May Ironside, Bob Marshall (in front), Leonard Halsall, Norman Kershaw, Tim Huyton, ?, Alan Chippendale, Jimmy Seddon, Roy Burnley, Bill Marshall, Tom Banks. *Seated*: ?, ?, ?, Edwin Kershaw.

tiny babies, brought the first horrifying realisation that no-one was secure from danger. Then the bewildered evacuees arrived in the district. These strangers, most of whom had no conception of life in the country, had to be accepted into the heart of the families of Scarisbrick and assimilated by the community – a very difficult process from all points of view. It was not made easier by the fact that the traditional family unit was already under stress as the menfolk were being conscripted and the young women were being directed either into the forces or into war-work. The enemy's objective of destroying the port of Liverpool, meant that a battle zone was very close at hand and the wailing sirens truly meant that danger was imminent.

The bombs that fell in the area were not aimed at a specific target in Scarisbrick. Although there was a radar station in Moorfield Rd, there was no real attempt by the Germans to destroy it. Nor did they target Bamber's Garage on Southport Rd, where munitions and DUKWS were made. Most of the bombs were intended for Liverpool, and either missed their target or were jettisoned as the German pilots turned for home. Nevertheless, the bombs that fell on Scarisbrick caused great concern at the time. One elderly resident still remembers the night a landmine fell near Primrose Hill. She was sheltering with her mother, crouched under the staircase, when they felt the ground shudder and then heard a terrific bang. They waited expectantly, wondering if the house was going to fall around them, and then crept to the window to see what had happened. They could see nothing but smoke. Unable to do anything more, they returned quickly to their shelter feeling extremely worried about the fate of some relations living in a little thatched cottage further down the lane. When morning came, they were greatly relieved to hear that their relatives had not been harmed.

Her father enrolled as a member of the Fire Guards and, after some basic training, was put on a rota to watch for any incendiary bombs that might fall during the hours of darkness and to deal with them. One night one fell by the brook behind their cottage on Jackson's Common. It flared up, illuminating all the nearby fields and cottages. Her father ran out with a spade to quench the flames by covering them with soil. As he did so, the German pilot brought his plane down low for a better view of the surrounding countryside. Fortunately, by the time the plane was near enough to see the panorama, the flames had been extinguished and the pilot could see neither the cottages nor the brave man who had foiled his plot.

Another large bomb fell on Bescar station yard. It fell directly on top of a ramp paved with stone sets. The ramp was alongside the railway lines, and was used by farmers when they brought wagons full of loose produce to tip into the railway trucks for transport to market. After the explosion the sets flew everywhere. One actually went through the roof of Wilf Taylor's house and fell on to the bed where he and his wife were sleeping. They suffered from severe shock, but were otherwise unharmed. The railway lines twisted up to a height of seventeen feet and one of the wagons was lifted and dropped on end inside another one. The contents of the wagons, coal, manure and every kind of produce were scattered everywhere. A corner of one of the wagons was broken off and, as it flew through the air, it narrowly missed George Ainscough of Station Farm. Certainly that night the German pilot succeeded in disrupting part of the English railway system, albeit not that centred at Liverpool, but nonetheless, an important rural district line that conveyed fresh vegetables to various urban centres.

Other bombs were less successful in reaching their targets. A clutch of ten bombs straddled the Scarisbrick countryside – some falling in the grounds of the Hall, some on Sutch's farmland, some in Black Moss Lane – but the only casualty was a rabbit. Another bomb was jettisoned on to Ashurst's Farm, but again nothing was harmed. Yet another bomb fell on a row of cottages in Cut Lane and damaged them so much that the tenants had to move to the school house at Halsall, while their homes were being repaired, but no-one was seriously hurt.

During the war every building in Scarisbrick was pressed into some kind of war service. As we have seen Scarisbrick Hall became a hospital for wounded soldiers, but nevertheless, the grounds continued to be used for events such as sports days and agricultural shows. Units from the services were often persuaded to show off their skills. In fact at one show the National Fire Service gave a display which is still remembered by those who saw it. The club in the tea-room at the post office opposite the Morris Dancers, was also commandeered and used as the head-quarters of the special constables; while the institute was used for First Aid Classes and as a centre for the Home Guard.

Meanwhile those who had not gone to serve in the forces struggled to make the land as productive as possible. Anyone who could lend a hand was welcome. As we have seen, the local children worked in the fields and, when increased food production became a vital issue, the Land Army established a camp in Summerwood Ave. behind the Parish Church in Halsall. The girls were drafted to Scarisbrick farms to work in the fields. They became indispensable to the farmers – so much so that several of them married farmers and stayed in the district after the war.

Other help came from both German and Italian prisoners of war. The Italians wore burgundy-coloured uniforms with a yellow patch on the back, and many were stationed at Wimbrook House in Aughton. The Germans lived at Aughton Hall or at a centre in Kirkby. They were brought to the farms in trucks with their own provisions and a guard, to help with seasonal work, and when evening came they re-turned to their camp. Some farmers needed more permanent help, and so one or two trusted prisoners were drafted to the farm to live on the premises for as long as they were needed. Everyone helped in the effort to produce more food. Even the smallest back garden was dug up to grow vegetables, while those who had any spare outhouses, turned their hands to rearing pigs.

When at last peace came, there were great celebrations in the village, including a huge bonfire party in the grounds of the Hall. Everyone thought that life in the village would return quickly to what it was in pre-war days, but that was not to be. Rationing continued and some foods were even harder to obtain than in wartime. Many of the menfolk eventually returned, but the loss of those who did not was deeply felt by their families. As a token gesture of gratitude to those who had fought, the Institute in Bullens Lane was converted into an ex-servicemen's club, where men could relax in the company of those who had experienced similar traumas to their own in the various war zones. At the instigation of Sir Everard a bar was introduced and ex-servicemen joining the club were charged no subscription for the first year.

Then in 1945 the news broke that the Hall and estate were to be sold. The Scarisbrick family's ancient ties with the village were to be broken. Those who worked on the estate were devastated. No longer would the gamekeepers be needed to keep the poachers at bay and to prepare for the next shooting party. No longer would the grounds be available for sports days and shows. No longer would there be work for the women of the village as cooks, housemaids and so on. However, when the Hall became the home of St Katharine's Training College for Teachers that fear was dispelled – domestic workers would be needed. The college had been evacuated to Keswick for the duration of the war and its governors wanted a new base in Merseyside close to its original home in Liverpool. Part of the college remained at Derwent Hill in Portinscale, near Keswick, for field study courses, but the majority of students moved into Scarisbrick.

One ex-student remembers one very wet day during the summer of 1946, when the 1944–46 students and their parents gathered for a prize-day in the Hall. The first impression was that long, long straight walk up the drive from Southport Rd to the Hall. There were no carriages – even without stalwart tenants to pull them – that day. Wet and bedraggled they reached the entrance to the Hall and realised that the wetting had been well worthwhile. Miss Allen and her staff proudly showed the visitors around the new headquarters of the College, trying in vain to keep the procession moving past the glorious carvings in the oak room. Change had come, but perhaps now more people would be able to enjoy and appreciate the architectural treasures of the building.

Castle Lodge on the eastern perimeter of the grounds of the Hall was

By direction of Sir Everard T. Scarisbrick, Bart., J.P.

SCARISBRICK HALL

(5 miles from Southport and 4 miles from Ormskirk,
1½ miles from Bescar Lane Station, L M S Branch)

Messrs. HATCH & FIELDING, F.A.I.

Are favoured with instructions to Sell by Auction, on the Premises,

Commencing MONDAY, SEPTEMBER 17th, and four following days,
at 11 o'clock each day

A Portion of the Valuable

Contents of the Mansion

Comprising:

Oak Refectory Table, on cross stretcher supports, 16ft. x 5ft.
Antique Carved Oak Cathedral Shaped Font on Pedestal.
Carved Dutch Oak Court Cupboard, 6ft. 6in. wide.
A Valuable Suit of 17th Century Armour.
Angelus 88-Note Player-Piano, in Mahogany Case.
Empire Gilt Settees and Chairs.
English and Dutch Marquetry Tables, Bureau and Writing Desk.
Reproduction Black and Gold Lacquered Furniture.
Luxurious Three-piece Chesterfield Suites.
Brown Oak Library Bookcases, from 4ft. 6in. to 20ft. wide.
A Valuable Library of Books.
600 ounces Solid Silver, Foreign Silver and Electro-Plate.
A Collection of Valuable Pictures by Artists of Repute.
120 Lots of Household Linen Blankets and Window Draperies.
17th Century Oak Four Poster Bedstead, dated 1637.
A Magnificent All-Brass Four Poster Bedstead, designed by Pugin.
The Contents of the Private Chapel.
Valuable Bassett Lowke Miniature Railway, Gauge 1, electrically driven, complete on stagings,
with Rolling Stock, General Equipment and Scenic Effects.
Greenhouse Plants, including a small collection of Orchids, and other Items.

On View: THURSDAY, FRIDAY and SATURDAY, SEPTEMBER 13th, 14th and 15th,
from 10-30 a.m. to 4-30 p.m.

N.B.—The Stately TUDOR GOTHIC MANSION, seated in a handsomely timbered Park,
with lake, extensive stabling, garages, cottages, four entrance lodges and carriage drives,
courtyard and every amenity appertaining to an important country seat, with beautiful
pleasure grounds, Home and Cliffe's Farms, extensive outbuildings, valuable woodlands,
accommodation and building land, in all about 475 acres, is FOR SALE by Private Treaty

For further particulars apply to Messrs. Hatch and Fielding, Auctioneers and
Estate Agents, 341 Lord Street, Southport (Tel. 55301-2), or to Messrs. Buck,
Cockshott and Cockshott, Solicitors, 26 Hoghton Street, Southport (Tel. 5112).

63. The sale catalogue for the 1945 sale of the contents of the Hall.

demolished in the 1940s. This imposing castellated building was beyond repair and was pulled down, Wards were closed at New Hall Hospital as drugs, discovered during wartime research, reduced the number of cases of scarlet fever, diphtheria and other infectious diseases. By the 1960s the hospital had only two wards – a ward for children with infectious diseases and a ward for tuberculosis. As methods of treatment changed, the verandahs were glazed and geriatric patients were moved in to fill the vacant beds. Finally in the 1980s, the decision was made to close the hospital and transfer the remaining patients to Fazakerley. Now New Hall hospital has been demolished, but perhaps the gate posts will remain, like the cast iron ones of the old fever hospital in Moss Lane to remind passers-by of that long-gone, much-valued institution of Scarisbrick.

For many years, the police were based opposite the Morris Dancers. The sergeant lived in part of the house and his three constables lived nearby in rented accommodation. It was police policy not to allow constables to buy property so that they could easily be transferred to other locations. The Scarisbrick station was, what was known as, an hourly one, because the Force guaranteed that it would be manned by constables on the hour, but at other times, the men would be out on the beat. The area it policed was very extensive, stretching from Halsall in the south to Banks in the north, so the men were kept very busy and it was impossible to man the station more frequently. Many re-member Police Constable Armfield who was stationed in the area in the 1950s, walking or cycling around the district, always in close contact with the villagers. Much of the constables' time was spent on traffic duty at the junction of Southport Rd. and Bescar Brow Lane before the traffic lights were installed, especially in the summer time and during rush hours.

The outcome of one traffic accident will long be remembered by the local police. It resulted in a man suffering a severed artery and needing immediate treatment in hospital. While Constable Armfield was attend-ing to the injured man and stemming the bleeding, the anxious onlookers suddenly saw an ambulance approaching. With great relief they flagged it down. When it stopped, they were dismayed to find that it was transporting six mothers with their day-old babies to another hospital. The man's plight was far more urgent, so the mothers and babies were crowded into the tiny police station. The ambulance

64. The Castle Lodge outside Scarisbrick Hall.

speeded away with the victim of the accident, leaving the constables to cope with the tiny babies and their mothers.

Another incident concerning the police happened on Coronation Day in 1953. A celebration dance was held at St Mark's School, and the dancing continued until the early hours of the morning. Then two exhausted, happy girls had to cycle home and their route was along the remote part of Moss Lane. Suddenly, two dark forms jumped out from the bushes, frightening the girls to death. It was a couple of young constables on their nightly patrol ready to escort the two young ladies safely to their homes.

Life on the mosslands was changed drastically in the 1950s by the installation of an extensive new drainage and pumping system. Drainage systems had been altered and installed throughout the ages, but this was the first reliable system. At last the farmers could plant with some confidence that they would reap a harvest. Previously flooding had occurred so regularly that many farmers had been forced to leave their mossland farms faced with huge losses.

There have been many changes in village life since the 1950s. The crematorium was built in the 1957–58 to cater for the needs of the area. The College left and Scarisbrick Hall school was opened by the late

65. Other memories of Sutch's Farm opposite Scarisbrick Park woods. *Left to right*: Stan Tinsley, Joseph Cropper, Bill Marshall on an Oliver 70 tractor 1946.

66. At one of the later Scarisbrick Agricultural Shows in 1949. *Left to right*: Mrs Robert Marshall, Mr Robert Marshall, Mr Ernie Shacklady, Mr William Cropper, Mr Joseph Cropper.

Mr Oxley. Tesco's store opened and, more recently, closed to move outside the Scarisbrick boundary at Kew. In fact there are too many changes to list, but as they occurred during the lifetime of the majority of my readers, they can be omitted from this catalogue of memories.

Before I close, there are one or two memories of the places and people of old Scarisbrick I would like to share with those who have lived in Scarisbrick for several years. Do you remember the bicycle shop where Ormsby's Church Furniture factory is situated? It belonged to Mr Marshall and later to 'Tag' Johnson and they used an old tramcar with its wheels removed, as a workshop. Do you remember Mr Chippendale, the shoe-repairer at the corner of Smithy Lane and Southport Rd and his assistant, George Thomas, who later took over the business successfully, despite being both deaf and dumb? Do you remember Dyson's mineral water factory which later became a cheese factory and is now a pine strip shop? Many of their bottles still containing a marble instead of a cork, are found in the fields and gardens nearby. Do you remember the four cottages known as Saddlers' Row behind the old police station? Do you remember the Post Office on Southport Rd, near Turning Lane where Mr Prior sold everything from bacon to paraffin? The list of memories is endless, and more are being accumulated as Scarisbrick faces the challenges posed by the dawning of a new century. No doubt there will be more sorrows and many celebrations, but I am confident the people of Scarisbrick will come through – as their predecessors hoped at the time of Queen Victoria's Diamond Jubilee – 'united in bonds of true amity and friendship', as they have done through out their long fascinating history.

Epilogue

OW I WOULD LIKE TO THANK all those people of Scarisbrick, especially those of the older generations, who have helped me to compile this history. Without their help, I would have been unable to make the past come alive.

I also owe a debt of gratitude to the Parish Council who initiated the compiling of this history of Scarisbrick in the first place, and whose endless encouragement has enabled me to bring the work to a successful conclusion. Then I must thank the staff of the Lancashire Record Office for their endless patience with my queries. My fellow historian and friend Audrey Coney has always been ready to help whenever a problem arose, but my greatest debt of gratitude is owed to my husband, who has processed photographs for me, controlled my wayward computer, and generally has supported me every inch of the way towards the completion of *A History of Scarisbrick*. Thank you all.

NOTES

Chapter One, *The Early History of the Township*

1. Morris, Chris (ed.), *The Journeys of Celia Fiennes* (London: Cresset Press, 1947), p. 184.
2. The activities of the many unique characters who have lived through this later period, would make a study in their own right, while those whose efforts resulted in the foundation of the WI, the Boys Brigade, the Guides and Brownies and in the building of the Village Hall, will be remembered well by the many Scarisbrick people who have benefited from their exertions, and who are still alive to describe their achievements.
3. 'Final Concords', Part I, R.S.L.C., vol. 39 (1899), p. 76.
4. The other townships are Skelmersdale, Bickerstaffe, Burscough, Lathom and Ormskirk.
5. V.C.H., III, pp. 265–75.
6. For Cockersand Cartulary, see C.S., vol. 43, New Series (1900) and for Burscough Priory Cartulary see C.S., vol. 18, Third series (1970).
7. A. Coney, 'Fish Fowl and Fen; landscape and economy on seventeenth-century Martin Mere', *Landscape History*, vol. 14 (1992).
8. J. M. Steane, 'Excavations at a moated site near Scarisbrick', T.H.S.L.C., vol. 112 (1960), pp. 147–53.
9. V.C.H., p. 268.
10. W. Farrer, *Final Concords of the County of Lancashire, Part IV, 1510–1558*, R.S.L.C., vol. 60 (1910), p. 51.
11. F. H. Cheetham, 'Two inventories at Scarisbrick Hall, Ormskirk, 1608 and 1673', T.H.S.L.C., vol. 89 (1937), pp. 123–38.
12. L.R.O. DDSc 26/34.
13. P.R.O. DL 30/79/1060.
14. F. Childrey, *Britannia Baconia . . .* (London: F. Childrey, 1661), p. 166.
15. Lancashire County Museums published a detailed guide by Rachel Hasted in 1984.
16. V.C.H., pp. 271–2.
17. Mr Edward Vose, the farmer who cultivated the land in the twentieth century, claimed that he had found broken gravestones when he was ploughing. He also unearthed a well-constructed tunnel nearby and at the time, there was much speculation as to its purpose.
18. Rev. W. T. Bulpit, 'Notes on Southport and District' (Southport: Southport Visiter, 1908), p. 179.
19. Royalist Composition Papers, Part III, R.S.L.C., vol. 29 (1894), pp. 88–90.

20. V.C.H., p. 274.

21. B. G. Blackwood, 'Parties and Issues in the Civil War', *Seventeenth-Century Lancashire*, T.H.S.L.C., vol. 132 (1983), pp. 103–26.

22. J. J. Bagley, *The Story of Merseyside*, Part II (Liverpool: Tinling & Co., 1969), pp. 22–6.

23. V.C.H. note p. 274.

24. L.R.O. QSB 1/272/16.

25. L.R.O. QSB 1/272/15.

26. L.R.O. QSP 31/32.

27. L.R.O. QSP 79/15.

28. L.R.O. QSP 331/15.

29. L.R.O. QSP 335/22.

30. L.R.O. QSP 416/13.

31. L.R.O. QSP 299/20.

32. L.R.O. QSP 303/16.

33. L.R.O. QSP 31/13.

34. W. Charlton, 'Touch Pieces and Touching for the King's Evil', T.L.C.A.S., vol. 31 (1931), pp. 32–3.

35. L.R.O. QSP 331/5.

36. L.R.O. QSP 416/7.

37. L.R.O. QSP 416/6.

38. L.R.O. QSP 35/25.

39. L.R.O. QSP 416/14.

40. L.R.O. QSP 307/1, QSP 307/9.

41. L.R.O. QSP 191/11.

42. L.R.O. QSP 303/14.

43. L.R.O. QSP 586/13, QSP 590/23.

44. L.R.O. QSP 335/13.

45. L.R.O. QSP 444/45.

46. L.R.O. DDSc 26/33.

47. L.R.O. QSP 35/29.

48. F. H. Cheetham, 'The Records of the Court Baron of North Meols 1640 & 1643', T.H.S.L.C., vol. 84 (1932), p. 17.

49. L.R.O. DDK 1521/3.

50. L.R.O. PR 2816. The Town Book of Scarisbrick.

51. This book is in the archives at Douai Abbey, Woolhampton. Robert also recorded 'the landmarks lettered August 5th 1732'. The lettering on the present stone milestones in Scarisbrick probably date from this date. Every effort should be made to preserve them.

52. L.R.O. DDSc 143/23.

53. L.R.O. DDSc 143/23.

54. L.R.O. PR 2816.

55. H. Broderick, 'Martin Mere'. Presidential Address to the Southport Society of Natural Science, 1902, p. 12.

56. It is interesting that Nicholas Blundell called on Robert Scarisbrick at the

time of the hearing and recorded, 'Mr Scarisbrick went out after dinner upon business about Martine Meer'. Tyrer, *The Great Diurnal of Nicholas Blundell*, R.S.L.C., vol. II (1970), pp. 97–8.

57. H. C. Collins, *Lancashire Plain and Seaboard* (London: J. M. Dent & Sons, 1953), pp. 60–3.

58. The figures quoted here are those quoted by Herbert Collins, but I would suggest that a more realistic measurement of the lowering of the sill was five feet.

59. L.R.O. DDSc 10/15.

60. F. Tyrer, *The Great Diurnal of Nicholas Blundell*, 1712–19, R.S.L.C., vol. II (1970), pp. 207, 226, 240.

Chapter 2, *Religion in Scarisbrick*

1. J. Evans (ed.), *Ormskirk Parish Church, a Guide and Short History* (revised 1990), p. 19.

2. The images might have been the Stations of the Cross. Dom. F. O. Blundell, *Old Catholic Lancashire*, vol. 3 (London: Burns, Oates and Washbourne Ltd, 1941), p. 46.

3. B. G. Blackwood, *The Lancashire Gentry and the Great Rebellion 1640–1660*, C.S., 3rd Series, vol. 25 (1978), pp. 121–2.

4. M. Havran, *The Catholics in Carolian England* (Stanford University Press, 1962), pp. 96–7.

5. L.R.O. QSP 509/31.

6. F. H. Cheetham, 'The Case of Robert Scarisbrick of Scarisbrick Esq. 1701', T.L.C.H.S., vol. 88 (1936), pp. 143–57.

7. J. A. Myerscough SJ, *A Procession of Lancashire Martyrs and Confessors* (Glasgow: John S. Burns & Sons, 1958), p. 191–3.

8. H. Foley, *Records of the Society of Jesus*, vol. V (London: Burns & Oates, 1879), p. 332.

9. The books which belonged to him – now at Douai – have had his name obliterated and the initials S.M. inscribed on the page to indicate that he betrayed the priest.

10. This book is at Douai Abbey, Woolhampton.

11. F. Tyrer (ed.), *The Great Diurnal of Nicholas Blundell*, vol. I, R.S.L.C. (1968), p. 129.

12. This is the first farm on the left after the bridge on the way to Ormskirk from Scarisbrick.

13. 31 Geo. III c. 32.

14. C.R.O. EDC 5 1678, No. 9, Deposition of Richard Taylor of Bickerstaffe.

15. H. Fishwick, 'Commonwealth Church Survey 1650', R.S.L.C., vol. I (1878), p. 92.

16. M. Duggan, 'Urban Change in a Lancashire Market Town 1660–1800', Ph.D thesis, University of Lancaster, 1992, p. 6.

17. C.R.O. EDA 2/5.
18. *Southport Visiter*, 22 April, 1853.
19. Rev. B. Nightingale, *Lancashire Non-Conformity* (Manchester: Heywood, 1887), vol. 6, p. 268–9.
20. Recorded in the Lancashire County Union Report of 1826. Nightingale, *Non-Conformity*, p. 269.
21. *History, Topography and Directory of Mid-Lancashire* (Mannex & Co., 1854).

Chapter 3, *Education in Scarisbrick*

1. A. F. C. Beales, 'A Biographical Catalogue of Catholic Schoolmasters in England, 1558–1700, Part I, 1558–1603', *Recusant History*, vol. 7, no. 6 (Oct. 1964), p. 271.
2. *Palatine Notebook*, Dec. 1881 (Liverpool: Henry Young, 1881), p. 221.
3. A. F. C. Beales, *Education under Penalty* (London: Athlone Press, 1963), p. 200.
4. C.R.O. EDV 5, April 1761.
5. C.R.O. EDV7/1/201.
6. Rev. R. Hodgson, *Life of the Right Reverend Beilby Porteus Late Bishop of London*, 4th edn (London: T. Cadell & W. Davies, 1813), p. 60.
7. Charity Commissioners' Report on the County of Lancaster (1898), p. 2033.
8. Fishwick, 'Commonwealth Church Survey 1650', p. 89.
9. C.R.O. EDA 3/3.
10. L.R.O. QSP 219/8.
11. L.R.O. WCW, James Carr of Snape, 1721.
12. Charity Commissioners' Report (1898), p. 2033.
13. L.R.O. DDSc 26/55.
14. L.R.O. SMSb 1/1.
15. P.R.O. E2/265, No. 5044
16. L.R.O. SMSb 1/2.
17. P.R.O. E2/265, No. 5044.
18. See previous chapter. *Directory of Mid-Lancashire* . . . (Mannex & Co., 1854).
19. Fee grants were introduced in the Elementary Education Act, 1891.

Chapter 4, *Memories of Scarisbrick*

1. *Souvenir booklet*, p. 15. I wonder if this valuable record and early example of the use of cine-photography still exists.
2. A. Mutch, *Rural Life in South West Lancashire 1840–1914* (Lancaster: C.N.W.R.S., Lancaster University, 1988), p. 44.
3. L.R.O. DDSc 22/8

LIST OF SUBSCRIBERS

1 Mr Norman Bimpson, Ormskirk
2 Mr Graham Fairhurst, Telford
3 Mr N. Taylor, Bescar
4 Mrs Y. P. Kenyon, Scarisbrick
5 Mrs Olive Davies, Scarisbrick
6 G. Ashcroft, Mawdesley
7 —
8 Mrs G. Ashton, Scarisbrick
9 Mrs Maud M. Lowe, Scarisbrick
10 Mr & Mrs J. Cackett, Scarisbrick
11 Mr and Mrs V. and B. Bolger, Scarisbrick
12 Library, KGV College, Southport
13 Mrs C. S. Ascroft, Scarisbrick
14 Mr Peter T. Houghton, Scarisbrick
15 Dr Margaret Cropper, Mossley
16 Mr Patrick White, Burscough
17 Mr James Ball, Scarisbrick
18 Mrs Joan McLeod, Scarisbrick
19 —
20 Mrs Phyllis Molyneux, Scarisbrick
21 Mrs Joan Sephton, Scarisbrick
22 Mr and Mrs G. Houghton, Scarisbrick
23 Councillor and Mrs Tinsley, Scarisbrick
24 —
25 Mrs E. Lovelady, Scarisbrick
26 Kathleen Johnson, Scarisbrick
27 Ann Brown, Scarisbrick
28 Jim and Wendy Wright, Banks
29 John and Rae Cotterall, Southport
30 Mrs M. M. Jackson, Scarisbrick
31 Mr W. Scarisbrick, Scarisbrick
32 Dr and Mrs K. D. Foggitt, Scarisbrick
33 Mrs S. Cropper, Scarisbrick
34 Mr and Mrs M. H. Lesley, Scarisbrick
35 Mrs D. Wolstenholme, Marshside
36 Mr E. A. Olverson, Scarisbrick
37 —
38 Mr David Goldstraw, Scarisbrick
39 Mr John Hart, Scarisbrick
40 Mrs K. E. Griffiths, Scarisbrick
41 Mr and Mrs J. G. Houghton, Scarisbrick

42   Mr Alan Prescott, Southport
43   Mr A. Watkinson, Halsall
44   R. L. Lancaster, Scarisbrick
45   Miss R. J. Oxley, Scarisbrick Hall
46   —
47   Julia Daphne Sutton-Smith, Scarisbrick
48   Scarisbrick C. P. School, Pinfold Lane, Scarisbrick
49   Mrs M. A. Hargreaves, Halsall
50   Mrs V. A. Smith, Scarisbrick
51   Ashley James Oldfield, Scarisbrick
52   Mr James Sudworth Davies, Scarisbrick
53   Dr R. W. and Mrs A. F. M. Small, Scarisbrick
54   Mr W. O. and Mrs M. McGregor, Oshawa, Canada
55   Michael and Janet Moore, Scarisbrick
56   Mrs W. J. Flower, Scarisbrick
57   M. A. Tomlinson, Scarisbrick
58   Mr F. Heyworth, Southport
59   Mr William Sell, Scarisbrick
60   Mr G. F. Roby, Ainsdale
61   Mrs A. K. Freeman, Scarisbrick
62   Mrs W. A. Seddon, Scarisbrick
63   Mr and Mrs Richard Ball, Scarisbrick
64   Mr Frank Taylor, Scarisbrick
65   —
66   Mr Mark Joseph Charnock, Halsall
67   Mr John Halsall, Scarisbrick
68   Gerard and Margaret Swarbrick, Scarisbrick
69   Mrs Jean Pye, Scarisbrick
70   Mr Arthur Naylor, Scarisbrick
71   Mr Paul C. Lang, Scarisbrick
72   Mrs Lilian Charnock, Scarisbrick
73   Jack Banks, Scarisbrick
74   James and Glenda Topping, Berry House, Scarisbrick
75   F. W. and D. Fairclough, Scarisbrick
76   Mr Bernard Horner, Scarisbrick
77   Mrs W. D. Moores, Ormskirk
78   Mr & Mrs J. Parrott, Ormskirk
79   Thomas and Helena Mary Hurst, Scarisbrick
80   Ruth Hurst Vose, Scarisbrick
81   Mr James Edward Vose, Scarisbrick
82   Mrs Jean Tabron, Southport
83   Mr P. J. J. Tabron, Southport
84   Mr D. T. Tabron, York
85   Scarisbrick C. P. School, Scarisbrick
86   C. K. Rutter, Scarisbrick
87   Carole and Bob Sheehan, Scarisbrick
88   —
89   Mrs M. Ashcroft, Scarisbrick
90   Mr and Mrs J. Olverson, Southampton

91 Mr and Mrs J. Rimmer, Holmeswood
92 Mr and Mrs P. Rimmer, Scarisbrick
93 Mrs H. M. Holden, Rufford
94 Mrs D. A. Coultard, Scarisbrick
95 Mr and Mrs M. Forshaw, Scarisbrick
96 Mr John I. Houghton, Scarisbrick
97 Mr Thomas Dawson, Scarisbrick
98 Mr Alan W. Scarisbrick, Scarisbrick
99 Mr Andrew Horner, Scarisbrick
100 Mrs H. Marshall, Scarisbrick
101 Mrs H. Jennings, Scarisbrick
102 Mrs Jillian Hilton, Scarisbrick
103 Dr Michael Massam, South Shields
104 Mr Bernard Halsall, Parbold
105 Mr Bernard Halsall, Ontario
106 St. Mary's R. C. Primary School, Scarisbrick
107 Mr L. M. and Mrs J. E. Collins, Scarisbrick
108 Francis Vose, Scarisbrick
109 Gwen and Fred Wilkinson, Scarisbrick
110 M. Charnock, Scarisbrick
111 Alan Wright, Southport
112 Mr J. F. Pickering, Banks
113 Pam and Rod Jones, Scarisbrick
114 —
115 —
116 —
117 Mrs E. Culshaw, Scarisbrick
118 Mr Joseph Vose, Scarisbrick
119 Mr Barry Critchley, Halsall
120 Mr and Mrs B. Egglesden, Lydiate
121 Mrs Eveline Graham, Scarisbrick
122 Mr and Mrs M. Dee, Scarisbrick
123 Mr and Mrs W. A. Sutton, Scarisbrick
124 —
125 The Formby Family, Scarisbrick
126 Mrs D. Stewart, Scarisbrick
127 Lesley Cordon, Scarisbrick
128 Mrs Janet Mary Hinton, Southport
129 D. L. James, Scarisbrick
130 Rev. and Mrs David Benge, Scarisbrick
131 Geoff and Hazel Clarke, Scarisbrick
132 A. E. and J Sargent, Scarisbrick
133 Mr and Mrs M. A. Reilly, Scarisbrick
134 Geraldine Wilby, Aughton
135 Marion Miles, Scarisbrick
136 Mr and Mrs K. D. Bowden, Scarisbrick
137 Mr T. Banks, Scarisbrick
138 Mrs K. A. Brady, Ashurst
139 Mr J. Lloyd, Scarisbrick

140 —
141 Mr and Mrs G. Dobson, Scarisbrick
142 Mrs M. A. Le Caplain, Wigan
143 Mrs Hilda Massam, Scarisbrick
144 Mr and Mrs D. A. Laidler, Scarisbrick
145 Rev. J. L. Arkwright, Scarisbrick
146 Rev Geoffrey Scott, Worcester
147 Mr Robert Howard, Scarisbrick
148 Mrs A. Hesketh, Halsall
149 Mrs Dorothy Green (née Prior), Southport
150 Mrs G. H. Hankin, Scarisbrick
151 Mr J. W. Simpson, Scarisbrick
152 Mr Stephen Shakeshaft, Scarisbrick
153 Mr Geoff Humphreys-Roberts, Scarisbrick
154 —
155 Mrs S. D. McNab, Scarisbrick
156 K. H. and P. A. Birch, Scarisbrick
157 Mrs M. Callary, Scarisbrick
158 Mr E. Serjeant, Halsall
159 Mr G. Forshaw, Scarisbrick
160 Mrs Ellen Baldwin, Scarisbrick
161 Mrs Brenda Baldwin, Scarisbrick
162 Mr L. D. Rippon, Scarisbrick
163 Mrs G. Jackson, Scarisbrick
164 The Birkdale and Ainsdale Historical Research Society
165 Mr R. W. Baxter, Burscough
166 Mr & Mrs D. C. Rothwell, Scarisbrick
167 Richard Sn, Richard Jn, Sharron & Rebecca Marsden, Scarisbrick
168 Ivy and Eric Marsden, Ormskirk
169 John and Yvonne Marsden & Family, Halsall
170 Cynthia and Graham Kilpatrick & Family, Halsall
171 Mrs Joyce Parkinson, Scarisbrick
172 Mrs Marion Lea, Aughton
173 Mr Thomas Pilkington, Scarisbrick
174 Mrs Ann R. Phythian, Scarisbrick
175 Mrs Margaret Julia Lee, Prenton
176 Mr Kenneth Whalley, Scarisbrick
177 Mrs V. Young, Maghull
178 Dr M. J. Smithson & Dr R. S. Bramwell, Scarisbrick
179 Mrs E. Bycroft, Scarisbrick
180 Mr Paul J. Smith, Omskirk
181 —
182 Mr & Mrs P. S. Pedley, Southport
183 Mr & Mrs A. Blundell, Scarisbrick
184 Mr S. J. Park, Scarisbrick
185 Mrs Doris Campbell, Crossens
186 Mr and Mrs J. Harrison, Scarisbrick
187 Mr W. Field, Aughton
188 G. E. and D. Dickinson, Scarisbrick

189 Mr E. Mullis, Scarisbrick
190 Mrs I. Meadows, Scarisbrick
191 Clifford Huyton, Banks
192 Mr and Mrs M. J. Jane, Scarisbrick
193 Mr and Mrs K. Richards, Scarisbrick
194 Mr H. Lee, Scarisbrick
195 Corrine Teresa O'Keeffe, Scarisbrick
196 James R. Orrell, Scarisbrick
197 Mr David Andrew Overton, Ormskirk
198 Janet Lennon, Ormskirk
199 —
200 Mrs Margaret M. Williams, Scarisbrick
201 G. H. and B. Hillmen, Scarisbrick
202 C. W. Hedges, Scarisbrick
203 Max and Mary Jones, Scarisbrick
204 Mr A. Sumner, Scarisbrick
205 Mr R. Church, Scarisbrick
206 Mr Michael R. Bennett, Scarisbrick
207 M. A. and A. M. Branwood, Scarisbrick
208 Mr and Mrs Uwe Callesen, Scarisbrick
209 Mr John Bate, Southport
210 Mr Derek Frank and Mrs Yvonne Sylvia Ray, Scarisbrick
211 Mrs S. Haycock, Scarisbrick
212 Ainsdale Produce, Scarisbrick
213 Mrs Elsie Church, Scarisbrick
214 M. L. and J. L. Holgate, Scarisbrick
215 Mr and Mrs John Carson, Scarisbrick
216 Mr and Mrs R. Dagnall, Rainford, St Helens
217 Mrs J. Sourbutts, Scarisbrick
218 Mrs Edna Sherman, Scarisbrick
219 Mr P. W. Scarisbrick, Scarisbrick
220 Mrs F. Halsall (née Massam)
221 Mrs Lillian Alker, Ormskirk
222 Mr T. P. Parker, Scarisbrick
223 Scarisbrick Hall School, Ormskirk
224 Mr and Mrs P. Hale, Scarisbrick
225 —
226 Mr M. J. Birch, Lytham
227 Mr and Mrs D. M. Williams, Scarisbrick
228 Mr and Mrs B. W. Jackson, Scarisbrick
229 Ian and Merle Bradley, Scarisbrick
230 Jeff Blundell, Scarisbrick
231 Mr T. R. Mawdsley, Scarisbrick
232 Dorothy Elizabeth Foster, Churchtown, Southport
233 St Mark's C. E. Primary School, Scarisbrick
234 Elaine Gail Sephton, Scarisbrick
235 Councillor Jane McDermott and Dr Kentigern J. Haworth, Scarisbrick
236 Mrs Doreen Hind (née Lydiate), Southport
237 J. M. Virgoe, Parbold

238 T. D. Latto, Southport
239 Miss G. Bond, Halsall
240 Mr J. M. Houghton, Scarisbrick
241 Richard A. Chambers ARICS, Scarisbrick
242 Misses Mary and Margaret Core, Scarisbrick
243 Denis and Jennifer Marshall, Scarisbrick
244 Mr and Mrs Armstrong, Scarisbrick
245 James Mark Alexander Blundell, Scarisbrick
246 Mrs Cecilia Marr (née Massam/Swarbrick)
247 James Sharrock, Scarisbrick
248 Miss M. Wilford, Southport
249 Mr and Mrs P. W. Lansdale, Scarisbrick
250 Mrs Alice Lea (née Formby) and Mrs Rose Burrill (née Formby)
251 Miss W. E. Mayor, Scarisbrick
252 Dr Clive A. Glass, Scarisbrick
253 Mr and Mrs J. Waterworth, Scarisbrick
254 Trevor Rimmer, Southport
255 Mr and Mrs G. Goulden
256 Miss K. M. Dobson
257 Dr G. Sechiari, Ormskirk
258 Mr James R. Downham, Southport
259 Mrs Mary Ormsby, Scarsibrick
260 Miss Leadbetter, Coventry
261 Mrs Marie Elizabeth Gornell, Scarisbrick
262 Elizabeth Marie Gornell, Scarisbrick
263 Barry Michael Gornell, Scarisbrick
264 Miss L. M. Charnock, Scarisbrick
265 Mrs Linda McCusker, Halsall
266 Stephen and Judith Smith, Scarisbrick
267 Mrs Anne Ellison, Scarisbrick
268 Mr & Mrs W. F. Rigby, Scarisbrick
269 John & Muriel Holcroft, Scarisbrick
270 Bill, Chris & Lee Williams, Scarisbrick
271 Dr M. J. Molyneux, Ormskirk
272 Mr Dennis Sephton, Southport
273 Mr John Marshall, Southport
274 Mr E. A. Orritt, Scarisbrick
275 Honorary Alderman & Mrs Michael Cox, West Lancashire
276 —
277 Mrs E. Nettleton, Scarisbrick
278 Mr Colin M. Prescott, Scarisbrick
279 Mr and Mrs M. Chisnall, Scarisbrick
280 Mr Norman Tidd, Southport
281 Mr J. Fyles, Scarisbrick
283 Mrs P. Paterson, Ormskirk
284 Mrs Anne Ainscough, Scarisbrick
285 Mrs Carolyn A. Kilshaw, Southport
286 Mr Dennis A. Halsall, Parbold
287 Mr & Mrs M. R. Seddon and Michelle, Scarisbrick

288 Mr & Mrs John Seddon, Halton-on-Lune
289 Miss Lilian Ainscough, Scarisbrick
290 Mr Stanley Inman, Scarisbrick
291 Mr Chris Wilford, Scarisbrick
292 Mrs Lynda Critchley (nee Church), Ormskirk
293 Mr & Mrs McIntyre, Scarisbrick
294 H. E. Canner
295 D. J. Darke, Scarisbrick
296 Andrew & Brenda Egglesden, Scarisbrick
297 Mr G. C. White, Hesketh Bank
298 Mr M. T. Draper, Rainford
299 Mr Alan and Mrs Rosalind Clowes, Scarisbrick
300 Mr George J. Harrison, Scarisbrick
301 —
302 Mr Maurice R. Parry, Scarisbrick
303 Mrs A. M. Spencer, Tarleton
304 Mr John Walton Forshaw, Scarisbrick
305 —
306 Mr & Mrs Michael Tyrer, Scarisbrick
307 Mrs J. V. Bishop, Southport
308 Mr Geoffrey John Wright, Southport
309 Mrs J. M. Burrows, Ormskirk
310 —
311 Mrs M. E. Gaskell, Scarisbrick
312 Mrs Ellen Prescott, Scarisbrick
313 Miss Sarah Jane Thompson, Scarisbrick
314 Mrs Emmeline Sephton, Ormskirk
315 Mrs D. Watkinson, Burscough
316 Mr G. E. Moorcroft
317 Mrs M. Josephine Prescott, Scarisbrick
318 Mrs M. Aspinall, Scarisbrick
319 Charles & Jean Walsh, Scarisbrick
320 Mrs H. Edgar, Ormskirk
321 Mrs H. Matthews, Scarisbrick
322 —
323 Mrs Rosa Bennett, Scarisbrick
324 Mrs Olive M. Holmes, Southport
325 Mrs A. Moore, Scarisbrick
326 Mrs M. Chapman, Whitefield
327 —
328 Mrs Joan Prescott, Aughton
329 Mr G. H. Hammersley, Preston
330 I. B. Woods, Liverpool
331 Mr Rod McDonald, Scarisbrick
332 Mr Kenneth James Houghton, Scarisbrick
333 Philip and Eileen Howard, Scarisbrick
334 Mrs Glenys H. Clarke, Southport
335 Mr Frank Porter, Scarisbrick
336 Mr and Mrs W. Core, Scarisbrick

337 Mr Frank Woodcock, Scarisbrick
338 Mr Edwin Johnson, Scarisbrick
339 Jane and Kevin Marshall, Scarisbrick
340 Timothy and Susan Edwards, Mere Brow
341 Mrs June Dean-Golics, Burscough
342 Mr John A. Price, Scarisbrick
343 —
344 Mrs N. Banks, Scarisbrick
345 R. D. Griffiths, Scarisbrick
346 Mrs L. Taylor
347 Mrs M. A. Griffin, Scarisbrick
348 Mr A. M. Seddon, Scarisbrick
349 Mr David and Mrs Dorothy Ashcroft, Scarisbrick
350 Mrs J. S. Lyon, Scarisbrick
351 Mrs B. Caddick, Southport
352 Mr and Mrs P. Forshaw, Scarisbrick
353 Mrs Phoebe Stazicker, Tarleton
354 —
355 The Whittaker Family, Scarisbrick
356 —
357 Ann C. Stewardson, Stockport
358 —
359 Mrs N. Topping, Scarisbrick
360 Mr Harry J. Cole, Scarisbrick
361 Mr Geoffrey Eaves, Scarisbrick
362 Mrs J. Alker, Ormskirk
363 Mrs L. P. Fagan, Scarisbrick
364 Mrs Susan Marshall, Eccleston
365 Mr William T. Banks, Birkdale
366 Mr & Mrs C. Caulfield, Poulton-le-Fylde
367 Peter Michael Gornell (deceased), Scarisbrick
368 Mr Peter Smith, Scarisbrick